Philippians and Galatians

INTERPRETATION
BIBLE STUDIES

Philippians and Galatians

STANLEY P. SAUNDERS

Geneva Press
Louisville, Kentucky

Book design by Drew Stevens
Cover design by Pam Poll
Cover illustration by Robert Stratton

First edition
Published by Geneva Press
Louisville, Kentucky

This book is printed on acid-free paper that meets the American National Standards Institute Z39.48 standard. ♾

PRINTED IN THE UNITED STATES OF AMERICA

01 02 03 04 05 06 07 08 09 10 — 10 9 8 7 6 5 4 3 2 1

Library of Congress Cataloging-in-Publication Data

Saunders, Stanley P.
    Philippians and Galatians / Stanley P. Saunders.
        p. cm.—(Interpretation Bible studies)
    Includes bibliographical references.
    ISBN 0-664-50102-8 (alk. paper)
        1. Bible. N.T. Philippians—Criticism, interpretation, etc. 2. Bible. N.T. Philippians—Study and teaching. 3. Bible. N.T. Galatians—Criticism, interpretation, etc. 4. Bible. N.T. Galatians—Study and teaching. I. Title. II. Series.

BS2705.2 .S28 2001
227'.407—dc21   2001023665

Contents

Series Introduction

The Bible has long been revered for its witness to God's presence and redeeming activity in the world; its message of creation and judgment, love and forgiveness, grace and hope; its memorable characters and stories; its challenges to human life; and its power to shape faith. For generations people have found in the Bible inspiration and instruction, and, for nearly as long, commentators and scholars have assisted students of the Bible. This series, Interpretation Bible Studies (IBS), continues that great heritage of scholarship with a fresh approach to biblical study.

Designed for ease and flexibility of use for either personal or group study, IBS helps readers not only to learn about the history and theology of the Bible, understand the sometimes difficult language of biblical passages, and marvel at the biblical accounts of God's activity in human life, but also to accept the challenge of the Bible's call to discipleship. IBS offers sound guidance for deepening one's knowledge of the Bible and for faithful Christian living in today's world.

IBS was developed out of three primary convictions. First, the Bible is the church's scripture and stands in a unique place of authority in Christian understanding. Second, good scholarship helps readers understand the truths of the Bible and sharpens their perception of God speaking through the Bible. Third, deep knowledge of the Bible bears fruit in one's ethical and spiritual life.

Each IBS volume has ten brief units of key passages from a book of the Bible. By moving through these units, readers capture the sweep of the whole biblical book. Each unit includes study helps, such as maps, photos, definitions of key terms, questions for reflection, and suggestions for resources for further study. In the back of each volume is a Leader's Guide that offers helpful suggestions on how to use IBS.

The Interpretation Bible Studies series grows out of the well-known Interpretation commentaries (John Knox Press), a series that helps preachers and teachers in their preparation. Although each IBS volume bears a deep kinship to its companion Interpretation commentary, IBS can stand alone. The reader need not be familiar with the Interpretation commentary to benefit from IBS. However, those who want to discover even more about the Bible will benefit by consulting Interpretation commentaries too.

Through the kind of encounter with the Bible encouraged by the Interpretation Bible Studies, the church will continue to discover God speaking afresh in the scriptures.

Introduction to Philippians and Galatians

Two Passionate Letters from Paul

The author of 2 Peter, the first recorded commentator on the letters of Paul the Apostle, admits that "There are some things in them (Paul's letters) hard to understand, which the ignorant and unstable twist to their own destruction" (2 Peter 3:16). Most readers of Paul's letters today would affirm at least the first part of this sentiment. Trained biblical scholars still find plenty to argue about in Paul's writings. It is worth noting that the comment in 2 Peter occurs in the midst of an affirmation of the authority of Paul's writings. If Paul's letters continue to be discussed at length after nearly two millennia, it is first because they richly repay careful and repeated study, not merely because they pose difficult problems. If we are tempted to throw up our hands in despair at Paul's dense prose or his sometimes sophisticated, sometimes troubling readings of the Old Testament, we should remember that fresh readings—and even misreadings—of Paul's letters have provoked and

The journeys of Paul

> **Introduction**
>
> "Together these letters suggest something of Paul's passion for the gospel, as well as the depth and quality of his compassion and love for the congregations he has founded—his family in Christ."

1

abetted some of the most significant movements in the history of the church.

The letters to the Philippian and Galatian congregations illustrate well the passion and intensity of Paul's writing. Philippians is perhaps Paul's warmest letter, affirming the already close relationship between the Philippians and Paul with the language of partnership, joy, and humility. Galatians, on the other hand, reveals frustration and anger and lacks the expression of thanksgiving typically found near the beginning of Paul's letters. While Paul presumes a relationship of trust and respect with the Philippians, the tone of Galatians suggests that he thinks he may already have lost this community to an erroneous vision of the gospel (a perspective that was really not the gospel at all). These letters suggest something of Paul's passion for the gospel, as well as the depth and quality of his compassion and love for the congregations he has founded—his family in Christ.

> "There are some things in them (Paul's letters) hard to understand, which the ignorant and unstable twist to their own destruction."—2 Peter 3:16

Most of the New Testament documents were intended for oral presentation in the worshipping assemblies of the earliest generations of Christians. Some basic observations about Paul's writings may help us better appreciate these letters to the Philippians and Galatians. Paul wrote within the context of an oral culture not only in which his letters were read out loud as wholes—not in pieces and snippets as we customarily do today—but in which the audiences had been trained to construct and interpret good arguments and stories. Paul's congregations probably met in homes in groups of no more than sixty or seventy people. The letters may have been read, or "performed," and discussed in association with an evening meal. If the logic of Paul's letters seems elusive, it may be in part because we have not read them as they were meant to be read, and in part because we are not trained in the same rhetorical and logical conventions as were Paul and his audiences.

> "Study of the epistles isolated from their context is like reading the answers at the end of an algebra book without the corresponding problems."—Calvin J. Roetzel, *The Letters of Paul: Conversations in Context*, 4th ed. (Louisville, Ky.: Westminster John Knox, 1998), 79.

Paul's letters are sometimes referred to as "occasional" letters. This refers to the fact that Paul was not carefully crafting abstract philosophical arguments. He was a missionary pastor who wrote on the run, sometimes even while in custody, to address particular situations within his churches. It is also important to note that Paul's letters are part of an ongoing conversation. Paul is building on previous conversations and correspondence and in many cases responding to questions. Paul sometimes uses his opponents' proof-texts against them, offering complicated and sometimes surprising interpretations of the Old Testament.

At the heart of Paul's thinking is a worldview quite foreign to our way of thinking in North America at the beginning of the twenty-first century. Not only was Paul a bi-lingual (or even multi-lingual) Jew living during the high period of the Roman Empire, he was also deeply immersed in the "apocalyptic" traditions of ancient Israel. When we hear the word "apocalyptic" we often think of "the end time," or "the end of the world." Paul's apocalyptic thinking, however, was more oriented toward the revelation of God's presence within history than toward speculation about what might happen at the end of history. In other words, Paul holds to the revolutionary view that God has already dramatically invaded history and is now at work transforming and renewing the whole creation, restoring as one body in Christ those who once were enemies. Paul is no "pie in the sky" thinker, then, but a radical social critic who is challenging the fundamental assumptions about the world that governed daily life. If we fail to appreciate this foundational and radical (i.e., reaching to the root of things) character in Paul's writing, we will surely misunderstand both him and the gospel he preached.

Philippians and Galatians each offer significant glimpses of a passionate preacher and pastor. Together they also provide a compelling

---

Timeline: The Life of Paul

(All dates are AD; all dates are approximate)

10 Saul is born in Tarsus. As a young man, he goes to Jerusalem to study as a Pharisee under Gamaliel.

29–30 Crucifixion of Jesus

30–31 Stoning of Stephen; Paul's conversion on the Damascus road. He spends some time in the Syrian desert, preaches three years in Damascus, makes a brief visit to Jerusalem to meet Peter, sets up a base of operations in Antioch.

46–48 Paul's first missionary journey, with Barnabas, to Cyprus and Galatia

48–49 The Jerusalem Council

49–52 Paul's second missionary journey, with Silas and Timothy, through Asia Minor to Greece. Returns to Antioch.

53–57 Paul's third missionary journey, again through Asia Minor and Greece. Returns to Jerusalem.

57–59 Arrest in Jerusalem; imprisonment in Caesarea by Roman authorities.

59–60 Paul's voyage to Rome, followed by two years under house arrest in Rome.

62–65 Paul is martyred (beheaded) in Rome during Nero's persecution.

From Celia Brewer Marshall, *A Guide through the New Testament* (Louisville, Ky.: Westminster John Knox Press, 1994), 79.

portrait of a complex original thinker who probably was the most significant missionary of his day, a theologian and social critic of rare power and insight whose legacy continues to spark heated debate. Yet if we catch even a little of Paul's vision, we are likely to be transformed. We may find ourselves called, like Paul himself, to a fresh vision of what God is doing in the world and to participation in the crucified body of Christ.

Want to Know More?

About leading Bible study groups? See Roberta Hestenes, *Using the Bible in Groups* (Philadelphia: Westminster Press, 1983); Christine Blair, *The Art of Teaching the Bible* (Louisville, Ky.: Geneva Press, 2001).

About the Letters to the Galatians and Philippians? See Charles B. Cousar, *Galatians*, Interpretation (Atlanta: John Knox Press, 1982); William Barclay, *The Letters to the Galatians and Ephesians*, rev. ed., Daily Study Bible series (Philadelphia: Westminster Press, 1976); Fred B. Craddock, *Philippians*, Interpretation (Atlanta: John Knox Press, 1985); William Barclay, *The Letters to the Philippians, Colossians, and Thessalonians*, rev. ed., Daily Study Bible series (Philadelphia: Westminster Press, 1975).

About the writings of Paul? See Calvin J. Roetzel, *The Letters of Paul: Conversations in Context*, 4th ed. (Louisville, Ky.: Westminster John Knox, 1998).

About the life of Paul? See Celia Brewer Marshall, *A Guide through the New Testament* (Louisville, Ky.: Westminster John Knox Press, 1994), 72–81.

1

Joy and Thanksgiving for the Philippian Congregation

Let us imagine for a moment what it might have been like to be a member of a Christian community in Philippi near the middle of the first century. We are part of a tiny (nearly invisible), ragtag minority, made up mostly of people who, like the vast majority in Philippi and other cities of the empire, live in daily poverty. We depend on one another and on good relations with our neighbors and the governing authorities just to survive. We have heard the proclamation of a band of Jewish missionaries, led by Paul, that the God of Israel took human form and died on a cross

Philippi during Paul's travels

outside Jerusalem but was raised from the dead. This vision of God is fundamentally different from anything we have ever heard about gods before, even about the God of Israel. We also know that to proclaim this Jesus as "Lord" puts us at risk with the Roman authorities, who claim in their propaganda that peace, salvation, and justice (or righteousness) are all gifts of the emperor to the conquered world. Rome demands of us our faith (or loyalty), which is now complicated by our new loyalty to the God we know in the stories of Jesus Christ. We have continued to support Paul financially and spiritually as he pursues his mission in other cities; but now we hear that Paul himself has been arrested by the Roman authorities. He is writing to us from jail. What feelings would we have as we first heard this letter from Paul read aloud in our household church?

Philippians was written to address just this situation, to deal with the tensions and anxiety that inevitably arise when people hear disturbing news about their founding teacher. To address these needs, Paul goes back to the foundations, reminding his friends who God is, and what the gospel of Jesus Christ is about. He spells out the implications of the Gospels with regard to the particular strains felt within the congregation. He reminds them of the relationship they have had with him in the past, and he encourages them to continue to nourish it.

> "I thank my God every time I remember you, constantly praying with joy in every one of my prayers for all of you, because of your sharing in the gospel from the first day until now."—Phil. 1:3–5

Philippians 1:1–2: A Provocative Salutation

Contemporary readers of Paul's letters might be tempted to merely glance at the introductory greetings or skip them altogether, since the most prominent information found in them—names, places, and what appear to be formulaic greetings—presumably have little to do with the real meat of the letter. Paul's greetings do, in fact, follow a pattern that was typical for his day, yet they convey a wealth of information that alerts astute readers to the mood, purpose, and content of the whole letter. The greeting includes a "signature" that identifies the writer and his colleagues, an "address" naming the recipients, and the "greeting" proper (Craddock, 3, 11–14).

The signature in Philippians (1:1a) identifies Paul and Timothy as co-senders (Timothy is also named in the signatures of 2 Cor., Col., 1 and 2 Thess., and Philemon). We do not know whether Timothy actually had a hand in writing the letter itself, especially since Paul uses the first person singular "I" throughout this letter. According to Acts 16, Timothy was present with Paul at the founding of the Philippian church and made a later visit as well (Acts 19:22). At the very least, naming Paul and Timothy together identifies them as parts of a team and affirms Timothy's authority in preparation for his visit to Philippi (Phil. 2:19–24). Still more important, however, is the designation applied to both Paul and Timothy: "servants (or slaves) of Christ Jesus." Slavery, or servanthood, will play a prominent role in the letter, designating the human form taken by Jesus (2:7), as well as the attitude and practices of Timothy in his work with Paul (2:22). More generally, it suggests something of the fundamental self-understanding and orientation toward others that Paul wants to hold up for the Philippians to imitate. By naming himself and Timothy as slaves of Christ Jesus, Paul indicates that his identity and honor—a matter of crucial importance in Paul's world—are tied inextricably to Jesus Christ, the one who has made known God's true nature by taking the form of

> "Of all his Churches, the Church at Philippi was the one to which Paul was closest; and he writes, not as an apostle to members of his Church, but as a friend to his friends."— William Barclay, *The Letters to the Philippians, Colossians, and Thessalonians,* rev. ed., 9.

a slave and dying on the cross (2:6–8). As "slaves," Paul and Timothy belong to Christ Jesus; their calling and destiny correspond with his. Hardly a casual designation, the identification of Paul and Timothy as slaves takes on even more texture as we consider the situation of those to whom Paul writes.

The address (1:1b) has several components and, like the signature, appears at first glance to be simpler than it really is. "To all the saints" may sound as if it names the holiest of the Philippian Christians, those whose character is beyond reproach. The term "saints" did suggest something of the moral character of those who followed God faithfully, but at its primary level it refers to God's claim upon those whose lives are bound up with God in a covenant relationship. God's call and claim *separated* "the saints" from the world so that they might dedicate themselves to service and worship. This does not mean that they lived physically separate from the world, but that God rather than the world laid claim to their imagination, vision, and practices. They are "God's people" rather than "the world's people."

Paul also identifies the addressees more particularly as saints "in Christ Jesus" and "in Philippi." The phrase "in Christ Jesus" suggests that Christ is both the location in which the Philippians have rooted their identity and the source and sustaining power of their new life. Some scholars point to the ancient conception of "corporate personality" or "the one who stands for the many" in order to clarify this relationship. As the "new Adam" (Rom. 5:12–21; 1 Cor. 15:22, 45–49), Jesus is the founder of a new people or race, who together make up his body. For Paul, Jesus himself is the embodiment of God's distinctive holiness, i.e., God's oneness, righteousness, grace, and loving mercy. The saints are those whose lives are set apart and sustained in relationship to this kind of holiness, and whose lives, in turn, bring those same qualities to expression.

"In Philippi" designates the physical, social, and cultural setting in which the Philippian Christians will "work out 'their' salvation" (Phil. 2:12). In Paul's day, Philippi was a flourishing Roman city, an administrative center of the Roman Empire and a crossroads of commerce, culture, and religion (Craddock, 12). It was also the site of an infamous battle fought there in 42 BCE between Brutus and Cassius, the assassins of Julius Caesar, and the victors, Antony and Octavian (Bakirtzis and Koester). A decade after this battle, Octavian defeated his former ally, Antony, and took for himself the title Caesar Augustus. He also rebuilt Philippi as a military outpost, established its leadership from the ranks of Roman soldiers and colonists, and granted the city the legal rights equivalent to a Roman territory in Italy. Citizens of Philippi were considered citizens of Rome itself (Bockmuehl, 4). Thus the city would have displayed all the trappings of Roman military power and presence, as well as shrines and altars dedicated to the mother goddess Cybele, Isis, and other local deities.

This is consistent with what Acts tells us of Paul's ministry in Philippi. According to Acts 16:11–40, Paul's missionary team encountered a slave girl whose "spirit of divination" was a source of income for her owners. After casting out the demon that possessed the girl, Paul and Silas are dragged before the magistrates, identified as Jews, and charged with disturbing the peace and advocating traditions that threaten Roman custom. This, Paul's first recorded encounter with Roman judicial authority, leads to severe beating and imprisonment. Recent studies, moreover, suggest that Philippi, rather than Rome, may have been the place where Paul was eventually executed (Bakirtzis and Koester). Paul's self-designation and call to slavery in conformity with Christ Jesus is even more provocative if we consider Paul's history in the city along with the environs of the congregation—a city filled with the images of Roman domination.

Paul concludes the address to the Philippians with the phrase "with bishops and deacons," which contemporary readers may associate with ecclesiastical offices. In Paul's day, however, the structures of the church were not so well developed, and many scholars argue that official offices with designations such as these did not develop for another generation or two. At the time Paul wrote to the Philippians, the terms were in common use to designate overseers (the literal meaning of the Greek word translated as "bishop") and attendants in civic or religious organizations, especially those who had responsibility for collecting and managing funds (Craddock, 13). Later in the letter Paul will thank the Philippians for their financial partnership in his mission (4:10–20), and in 2 Cor. 8–9 he lifts them up as a model of generosity amidst poverty and suffering. It is likely, then, that Paul is thinking of those among the Philippians who have had a hand in bringing this aspect of their partnership in ministry to fruition.

The greeting proper (1:2) with which Paul closes the introduction to this letter names two foundational aspects of Paul's ministry—grace and peace through God in Jesus Christ. These terms may sound innocently religious and even bland in our ears, but in fact they were politically charged in Paul's day. The Greek word "charein," which meant something like "greetings," was a common oral and literary greeting. Paul alters the customary greeting and introduces all of his letters with "charis" (grace), which reminds his audience of their fundamental dependence upon God's grace. The word "peace," also found in the greeting of most of Paul's letters, recalls the Hebrew word "shalom," which speaks of the peace of God that had been promised to Israel through the prophets. "Peace" was also commonly used in Paul's day in reference to the benefits of the Roman Empire. Peace was the social ordering of life secured by Roman conquest. "Pax Romana," the peace and security of Rome, was in fact the motto of the Roman world after Octavian (Caesar Augustus) ended the civil war and established "universal peace" (Georgi, *Theocracy*, 28; see also Horsley, and Wengst, *Pax Romana*). In Philippi as in Rome, the word peace was laden with the associations of imperial rule. This context makes it all the more striking that Paul greets the Philippians not by affirming the "Peace of Rome," but by acknowledging the grace and peace that is from "God our Father and the Lord Jesus Christ." Caesar is neither god nor father, despite the claims of Roman imperial propaganda. For Paul there is but one God and Father, the one he knows from the traditions of Israel and from his encounters with Jesus Christ.

> "And this is my prayer, that your love may overflow more and more with knowledge and full insight, to help you to determine what is best, so that in the day of Christ you may be pure and blameless."—Phil. 1:9–11

Philippians 1:3–11: A Joyous Prayer of Thanksgiving

In the two introductory verses, Paul has already subtly introduced the key themes and images that will run throughout this letter. In the section that follows, 1:3–11, Paul offers thanksgiving for the Philippian Christians (which further evidences the deeply personal relationship he has with them), begins to speak of his and their current circumstances, and names the hope he has for them. With the exception of his correspondence with the Galatians, all of Paul's letters include a thanksgiving. Thanksgivings were also found commonly in other letters of the day. Paul adapted the common form for his own purposes, using the thanksgiving to reestablish a favorable relationship with his audience, which would make hearers more attentive and receptive to his message, and to lay out the primary themes he addressed in the rest of the letter (Murphy-O'Connor, 62ff.).

Throughout the thanksgiving section in Philippians, Paul's language breathes of joy, mutual affection, partnership, grace, and love—to all of which he later returns. He also mentions for the first time his imprisonment (1:7), which becomes the focus of the following section (1:12–26).

It would be a mistake, however, to reduce this thanksgiving to a "table of contents" or a rhetorical device designed to curry favor with his audience. At its most basic level, it is a heartfelt prayer that demonstrates Paul's exuberance for the gospel and is driven by his strong eschatological convictions—his sense of the way God has transformed life, both present and future.

Paul twice refers to the "day of Christ" (1:6, 10) and seems to understand it as a time of completion and judgment. We need to be careful, however, not to limit Paul's eschatological convictions to (future) temporal terms, or to speculate at length about whether he believed the world was about to end. Paul may indeed have believed that the final judgment was at hand, but if so, he believed it in large measure because of what God had already done and was now doing, both among the Philippians and through his own ministry. In other words, the world he had once known no longer held him captive; through God's transformation it was already coming to an end. Appropriately, then, Paul's thanksgiving focuses first on the past, remembering what God has done (1:3–6), then on the present (1:7–8), and finally on the future, Paul's hope for the Philippians in the day of Christ (1:9–11) (Craddock, 16–21).

"In circumstances which could understandably breed doubt, despair, even bitterness, Paul remembers and is grateful. . . . Paul already knew before conversion that being a believer is to a large extent an act of memory. It still is, as some early Christians understood when they referred to being lost in the world as "having amnesia."—Fred B. Craddock, *Philippians*, Interpretation, 16.

While this thanksgiving anticipates what is yet to come, Paul's language immerses his audience in an extravagance of grace that transcends the human boundaries of time and place, testifying to his perception of how far God's grace reaches into human experience: "constantly praying with joy in every one of my prayers for all of you" (1:4); "your sharing in the gospel from the first day until now" (1:5); "all of you share in God's grace with me" (1:7); "I long for all of you with the compassion of Christ Jesus" (1:8); "that your love may overflow more and more" (1:9), all yielding "the harvest of righteousness, that comes through Jesus Christ for the glory and praise of God" (1:11). Because the past, present, and future are filled with God's grace ("charis"), thanksgiving ("eu-charis-to") is the appropriate response (1:3).

For Paul, God's grace also embraces disconfirming experiences, such as his imprisonment (1:7). While we do not know where Paul is in prison—Rome, Caesarea, or Ephesus are most often mentioned as possibilities (Osiek, 27–30; Bockmuehl, 25–32)—it is clear that he is in Roman hands, which suggests that he was facing serious charges and possibly lethal consequences. Paul mentions in

> "Nowhere in Paul's letters does one get the impression that his love waited for the phone to ring. We have no reason to doubt his sincerity when he says his love is the very love of Christ (v. 8) which was, of course, an initiating love, not a love reacting to the initiative of another."—Fred B. Craddock, *Philippians,* Interpretation, 18.

verse 13 that his imprisonment is "for Christ" and that, despite what some may think, his circumstances have led to the spreading the gospel and have made other brothers and sisters speak the word more boldly (1:12–14). Paul refers to the Philippians as "fellow sharers," "co-partners," or "co-fellowshippers," emphasizing the depth of their relationship with him (Craddock, 19). When Paul speaks the language of "koinonia," as in verses 5 and 7 (see also 2:1, 3:10, 4:14), he has something more in mind than the English translation "fellowship" has come to mean. He's not thinking of moments of easygoing friendliness or a casual meal with other church members, but of a deeply committed, honest, and even pain-filled involvement with one another. In this case, partnership/fellowship between Paul and the Philippians implies their complete identification with the gospel of Jesus Christ and with Paul's mission, whether that mission, or grace (as he calls it here), takes them with him to prison or to the courtroom, or involves their suffering and death (see 1:30, 3:10).

Partnership and mutuality are so powerfully at work here that at two points Paul's language seems to lose precision, to the effect that it is not clear in the Greek who is remembering or caring for whom. The clause in verse 3 that the NRSV translates "every time I remember you," could also read "every time you remember me"; and where the NRSV reads "because you hold me in your heart," in verse 7, one could also read (as did the RSV) "because I hold you in my heart." Most English translations and commentaries prefer "every time I remember you" or its equivalent in verse 5, but are more evenly divided in their judgments about verse 7. However one decides to translate these passages, it is clear that Paul is working very hard in this thanksgiving to describe a relationship of mutual caring and depth that few of us in our more individualistic, consumer-oriented culture of alienation would dare to imagine. For Paul, God's presence with us in Jesus Christ has opened up new realms of possibility for the way humans relate to God, to the creation, and to one another, making possible this kind of "partnership" (1:5).

To be sure, it is possible that Paul's extravagant language in this thanksgiving is not descriptive, but wishful. He may be calling the Philippians to a depth of relationship by describing it as if it were reality. There are, in fact, indications that some in the Philippian church have questions about what has happened to Paul and whether he is the kind of leader they ought to be following (1:12–18, 28). As the letter continues Paul deals with factions and conflicts that have developed among the Philippian Christians, which also suggests that the real picture is not as uniform and rosy as this thanksgiving suggests. Whether real or ideal, the vision Paul prays for takes us to the heart of Christian community—the full sharing and identification with one another, even in difficult, life-threatening circumstances when our commitment to the gospel places us at odds with the larger culture. Paul's task, in the letter to the Philippian church, is to provide guidance for living out this vision in first-century Philippi.

Want to Know More?

About the marks of the Christian life? See William Barclay, *The Letters to the Philippians, Colossians, and Thessalonians,* rev. ed., Daily Study Bible series (Philadelphia: Westminster Press, 1975), p. 13ff.

"[W]e can anticipate having to think through again issues of ministerial relationships, professional distance, the need to belong and yet the dangers of intimacy, and the whole question of what it is which characterizes relationships as Christians. Doctors and lawyers have clients and they have friends, but only ministers have congregations."—Fred B. Craddock, *Philippians,* Interpretation, 20.

? Questions for Reflection

1. Paul is attempting to help the Philippian Christians live faithfully in the context of the Roman Empire. What might it mean to live faithfully in the midst of a world power? What unique challenges does our own cultural context present us with as we seek to live faithfully? One of the characteristics of life in the twentieth century in North America is the celebration of individualism and economic self-interest. In what ways do these factors affect our understanding and practice of the Christian faith?

2. Fellowship is a word we frequently hear in Christian communities. Partnership is a term we commonly associate with the financial world. How are these terms used in your church? Review Paul's usage of these terms in Phil. 1 and explore their meanings in biblical encyclopedias and dictionaries. How might churches today reclaim the kind of partnership and fellowship Paul had in mind as he wrote to the Philippians?

3. What does the image of slavery convey in our cultural and historical experience? Using biblical encyclopedias and dictionaries, explore slavery in the first century. How is our understanding of slavery different from what Paul might have understood by this term? What would it mean for us to be "slaves of Jesus Christ"?

4. Spend some time exploring Paul's understanding of the end times (eschatology). How does this compare with eschatology as it has been popularized in our culture in books and videos and by media preachers? What is the significance for the church of the end times being present now in the transformative work of God?

2 Philippians 1:27–2:16

Shaping Christian Community around the Story of Christ

Paul begins the body of the letter by interpreting his imprisonment (1:12–26), which apparently was the source of concern to the Christian congregation. His imprisonment had provided an occasion for other preachers to pursue their own ambitions at Paul's expense (1:15–17). Paul responds to the concerns of the Philippians about the effects of his imprisonment on the Gospel with words of joy and assurance. His imprisonment, Paul proclaims, has allowed the Gospel to advance in three ways: 1) It is clear to those in Paul's immediate company that he is in bonds for Christ (1:13); 2) Others have been en*courage*d to preach the gospel with boldness (1:14); 3) Even though some are using this opportunity to compete with Paul, he rejoices in any proclamation of Christ (1:18).

Paul

But what about Paul and the church at Philippi? What is the future for Paul? What is the future for the Philippian community? Paul responds to this concern with an honest struggle between his hope to depart and be with Christ and his desire to be released. In the end, Paul asserts his certainty that he will be released to return to the community (1:25–26), only to reintroduce uncertainty in verse 27, where he moves to address the practical business of conduct within the community.

Phil. 1:27–30: The Politics of Life in a Hostile City

The Christian life in a city like Philippi at the time Paul wrote this letter would have been a risky undertaking at best. Given its status as a military colony, the attachments of its leading citizens to Roman political power, and its important place in Roman history, Philippi was a little "Rome away from Rome." To make their way in this environment and preserve their peculiar vision and faith-filled way of life, the Philippian Christians would need to support one another fully, reminding one another in both word and practice of what they held to be true—not the good news that Rome proclaimed, but the good news of Jesus Christ. Paul understands the Christian calling virtually as an alternative citizenship. What the NRSV translates as "live your life" (1:27) more accurately means "live out your citizenship" (Craddock, 33; Osiek, 47). In 3:20 Paul will use another form of this word when he says, "But our commonwealth (citizenship) is in heaven." In both cases the Greek terms used are forms of *polis* (city), which is the basis for the English word "politics." Paul is, therefore, not calling on the Philippians to live their faith in hiding to blend in with the culture; he is insisting that they adopt a new polity, a distinct way of organizing their relationships. That living this distinct citizenship may put the Philippians at risk is clear. The Philippians' witness to the gospel of Christ will threaten those whose loyalty is elsewhere.

A church that stands together with Christ at its center will be a sign, a demonstration of where history is heading in God's grace, and thus also a portent of destruction for whoever opposes

> "That which will make Paul's joy complete is concord and harmony in the church at Philippi. For emphasis as well as clarity he says what he has in mind in four expressions: being of the same mind . . . ; having the same love; being in full accord (joined souls); and of one mind (he repeats the call for a common attitude or mindset)."—Fred B. Craddock, *Philippians*, Interpretation, 36.

God's way in the world. There is no triumphalism implied here, as 1:29–30 makes clear—as the Philippian Christians live out their alternative citizenship they will be granted ("graced") the privilege of suffering for him, just as Paul himself has.

Phil. 2:1–11: The Politics of Christian Unity

Because Paul and every other Christian is a slave of Christ Jesus—not of Caesar nor any other human master—a wholly new foundation for human community is put in place. As Paul will make clear, the community that serves and honors Christ is no longer held captive to the ideology of alienation and division that is characteristic of the culture of the Roman Empire nor to the selfishness, conceit, and pursuit of self-interest (cf. 2:3–4) that are symptomatic of this ideology.

In 2:1–4 Paul repeats words from his thanksgiving: joy, partnership, love, affection, unity, and mindset or attitude (Craddock, 35). Despite the possible ambiguity in verse 1, with the English *if*, the syntax Paul employs implies an affirmation (i.e., "If there is any encouragement in Christ [and there is!], any consolation from love [and there is!] . . .). He is describing the experiences they have had as a foundation from which to build. When in verse 2 Paul calls upon the Philippians to "be of the same mind, having the same love,

> "Because in Jesus of Nazareth they experienced God, the Christians used pre-existence as one way of saying that in the very human, crucified Nazarene they had encountered reality beyond all contingencies of time, place, and history. The church has always proclaimed this paradox about Jesus Christ, but always with difficulty."—Fred B. Craddock, *Philippians*, Interpretation, 40.

being in full accord and of one mind," he has in mind the wholly new way of shaping identity and community—the alternative polity—that is already a part of their Christian experience. It is this pure, single-minded devotion to the gospel proclaimed and embodied by Christ that will unify the community in the face of its opponents. Paul's call to have one mind does not mean, however, that there is no room for diversity of thought or opinion within the community, nor that Christians will always agree on every topic. It does mean having a common attitude or orientation that he is about to define. Paul's fourfold directive and repetition of the concept of "same mind" (1:7; 3:15; 3:19, 4:2) makes it clear that discord has become a serious problem in Philippi, where this unity and common vision was being destabilized from within.

Paul begins his description of the Christian mindset by first identifying actions to avoid: "Do nothing from selfish ambition or conceit, but in humility regard others as better than yourselves. Let each of you look not to your own interests, but to the interest of others" (2:3–4). He then turns to the communal worship of the Philippians and the model of Christ to elaborate on this mindset.

Most scholars agree that verses 6–11 constitute a hymn, possibly a hymn sung during the Eucharistic (communion) meals. Using this communally held understanding of Christ, Paul reveals the attitude they are to have in common. The story told in the "Christ Hymn" remains the most foundational—and provocative—confession of the Christian faith we possess even after twenty centuries of Christian experience and reflection.

Although scholars analyze the structure of the hymn in a variety of ways, it seems to fall most naturally into two parts: verses 6–8, which tell the story of Jesus' incarnation, life, and crucifixion, and 9–11, which recount his exaltation. At the same time, one can discern in the hymn a line running from "pre-existence" (Jesus as divine) to "existence" (Jesus as human and slave) to "post-existence" (Jesus exalted) (Craddock, 40). While this may raise questions for some about the nature of Jesus' being, it is more important to affirm that in Jesus Christ the early Christians encountered one whose reality transcended the human constructs of time, place, and being (Craddock, 40). It is also important to hold the two parts of the hymn together as a unity. This requires that we understand its dual focus on self-emptying and humility, on the one hand, and exaltation, on the other hand, as a paradox. Within the lines of this hymn are held two seemingly contradictory elements that together make up a whole greater than the sum of its parts. In popular thought, the crucifixion is sometimes treated as a terrible mistake that God erases when Jesus is raised from the dead. This line of thinking, however, not only dissolves the paradox, but allows one too easily to skip past the suffering to which Paul keeps drawing the Philippians' attention. But even if one embraces suffering, it is still possible to misread the hymn as a model of "a little suffering now for the sake of exaltation later" (Craddock, 42). For Paul, however, the exaltation of Jesus confirms rather than negates his life of self-emptying for others and

> "So what Paul is saying is, 'You and I know full well the privileges and the responsibilities of being a Roman citizen. You know how full well even in Philippi, so many miles from Rome, you must still live and act as a Roman does. Well then, remember that you have an even higher duty than that. Wherever you are you must live as befits a citizen of the Kingdom of God.'"—William Barclay, *The Letters to the Philippians, Colossians, and Thessalonians*, rev. ed., 30.

> "Is there not the danger of work slipping over the line into work righteousness? That danger has apparently driven some members and clergy straight to the hammock as the only place where a doctrine of grace can be kept safe."—Fred B. Craddock, *Philippians*, Interpretation, 46.

his servant's death on the cross. It says, in other words, that Jesus' way of life—the way of self-emptying, solidarity with the humiliated, and crucifixion—is what God affirms and exalts. It is on the cross of Jesus Christ, in fact, that God's glory is most powerfully evident.

The hymn clearly models the denial of self-interest, as well as the divestment of divine (and human) status and privilege. It does not say, however, that Jesus gives up his divine identity. Instead, he expresses it perfectly by becoming a slave. This important nuance allows us to affirm Jesus' full divinity and full humanity at the same time. But more than this, it means that by becoming human, a slave, and finally by being crucified, Jesus demonstrates for us who God really is.

The Politics of Humility and Obedience

The hymn also speaks of Jesus "humbling himself" and "becoming obedient" (2:8). We usually understand "humility" as a personal virtue, akin to meekness and modesty. These are perfectly good virtues, but the word Paul uses here really signifies the act of placing oneself in solidarity with the humiliated (Wengst, *Humility*), that is, complete identification of oneself with those who huddle together on the broken, bottom rungs of the human ladder. Solidarity with the humiliated is not the same as solidarity with the humble. Lots of us consider ourselves humble—we may even be proud of our humility and prefer to associate with other humble people. But we aren't the humiliated of this world—the poor, the outcasts, those we cross the street to avoid. When Jesus comes into this world as a slave, he embodies God's complete identification with the humiliated, precisely what Paul wants the Philippians to practice in their life together in place of the self-serving behaviors that characterize life in the fallen creation. The kind of "humility" Jesus demonstrates for us fundamentally undermines worldly perceptions and expressions of power, and thus represents a radical subversion of the way life was structured in the Roman Empire (as well as today!).

Want to Know More?

About works, grace, and salvation? See Shirley Guthrie, *Christian Doctrine*, rev. ed., (Louisville, Ky.: Westminster John Knox Press, 1994), chapter 16.

In his denial of privilege, his taking on the form of a slave, his identification with the humiliated, and finally in his death as a criminal on the cross, Jesus demonstrates his obedience to God. Many people in modern North American culture may be offended by the language of obedience, perhaps because we so often live in unwitting obedience to the individualistic, "I'll do what I want" ethos of our day. In contrast, the question asked by people of Paul's day was not if one would obey, but who one obeys. Paul was aware that all of us submit, whether knowingly or not, to the "principalities and powers," the dominions, the demons, and the other spiritual forces of this world (Craddock, 41). In becoming fully human, Christ Jesus places himself under the power of these hostile forces, even the power of death (Gal. 4:3–4, 1 Cor. 2:8). Not even Caesar could avoid obedience to this power. But when God raises Jesus from the dead, exalting him and giving him the name above every name (2:10), even the power of death is broken. For precisely this reason, Paul has no reason to fear death (1:20–24), or any other power of this world, whether human or spiritual. For the same reason, the Philippians have no reason to fear any human power, whether it be the opponents among their neighbors in Philippi or the powers of Rome. Because of his conquest of the powers of this world, including death, Jesus now offers to redeem—to set free from bondage—those who put their trust in him completely and without limit.

Isaiah's Vision and the Politics of the Christ Hymn

Redemption from the powers of this world is never far from view, even if it is not explicit in the words of this hymn. The whole Christ Hymn resonates deeply with language and imagery of Isaiah 40–55, especially with Isaiah's vision of the "suffering servant," whose suffering redeems others. Jewish people understood the servant not merely as an individual person, but as a figure who symbolized the redemptive suffering of Israel itself. As a consequence, they would have understood that the hymn tells the story not only of Jesus, but of the suffering, redemption, and redemptive power of all of God's people.

The resonance between the hymn and the collective imagery of Isaiah is particularly evident in the language of verses 10–11, which is borrowed from Isaiah 45, where the prophet sets forth the last days vision of God's vindication of suffering Israel and the gathering of the nations to worship God. Isaiah 45:23 says that at God's name every knee will bow and every tongue confess. But here in the Christ Hymn, Jesus' name stands for the name of God. In other words, Jesus is given "the name"–not just the name "Jesus" or "Lord," but the "holy name": Yahweh (Bauckham, 131; Bockmuehl, 145). Isaiah's vision (and Paul's) associates this naming with the gathering of the nations to worship Israel's God. This, in fact, is the very reason why Paul pursues his mission among the Gentiles: he is announcing to the nations that the Lord is none other than Jesus Christ. His congregations are the sites where the nations are gathering, as Isaiah envisioned. And that, in turn, is why we still gather in congregations today to tell the story of Jesus. This hymn is not only Jesus' story, nor only the Philippians' story, but our story, too.

As we reflect upon Paul's use of this hymn, it will be helpful to recall the context in which he writes. We already know from the letter that Paul is a prisoner of the Roman authorities when he writes to the Philippians. Imagine a prisoner, one who faces the possibility of being executed by the Roman state, writing about Jesus, who does not consider equality with God as something to hold on to, or to exploit, but empties himself, not only taking the form of a slave, but dying the death of a slave on the cross. For Paul this could hardly be just an interesting theological point. He's talking about life and death, Jesus' death and his own. In this hymn, then, he holds up the life of Jesus for everyone in the Philippian church to see, and says this kind of life is what the real Lord of the universe honors. Knowing Paul's own situation as prisoner and self-proclaimed slave of Jesus Christ makes his citation of the hymn all the more poignant and powerful.

Phil. 2:12–16: The Politics of Grace

The Christ Hymn brings into focus the drama of salvation, which here is the story of God entering the world in solidarity with the least ones and being put to death on the cross as a criminal slave, to free all of creation from the fallen powers. This is precisely the reality to which Paul points in the words that immediately follow the hymn itself (2:12–16). As Jesus patterned his life in obedience to God, so, too, Paul patterns his life in obedience to Christ, and now calls upon the Philippians to continue to pattern their life together in obedience to him, regardless of whether he is present with them or absent (2:12). In this way, the ministries of Christ, Paul, and the Philippians are joined together as one, in imprisonment and trial, in suffering, and in hope of resurrection. While their obedience is rooted in God's grace, it nonetheless requires that they "work out their salvation in fear and trembling," that is, in reverence before God, the only true power of Creation. Two observations follow. First, this passage is one of many that challenge conventional Protestant notions of a grace that requires no work. Grace and works are not opposites in Paul's thinking. To be sure, we cannot earn our salvation. On the other hand, God's grace sets us free to work as we have never before imagined for the sake of God's redemptive reign (Craddock, 46). Second, it should be clear from this passage that Paul's understanding of salvation is different from what many of us have learned in church. Salvation is not a matter of never sinning, or never touching those we consider unclean. Nor is it a matter of having our sins taken away and joining the ranks of a comfortable middle-class congregation. Salvation consists, rather, in the joy, freedom, and partnership we experience when God's grace sets us free from the powers of this world, not so that we can flee this earth, but so that God can use us "to work for God's good pleasure" (2:13), and so that we can "shine like stars" (2:15) in the darkness of a broken world that God is preparing for redemption.

> Paul's use of the term "slavery" to characterize the relationship with Christ may make contemporary readers uncomfortable. Paul sounds like someone who has given himself up entirely for another and no longer has a clear identity of his own. To be sure, Paul would not be very much at home in our individualistic culture. His way of expressing his relationship with Jesus Christ is at home, however, in Mediterranean culture, which typically shapes identity in relationship to central figures—the householder, one's master or father, the patron of a community, or Caesar, for example. Thus, Paul's denial of self and focus on Christ is what one would expect of a slave in relation to the master.

When we read and sing together on Palm Sunday this audacious Christ Hymn about the God who is a slave and a slave who is God, we would do well to remind ourselves that as we do so, we are being called to join ourselves to Jesus, to Paul and the Philippians, to all who through the grace of God commit themselves to this way of life. In lives so committed, we offer more perfect praise to God.

> "The story told in the "Christ Hymn" (2:6–11) remains the most foundational—and provocative—confession of the Christian faith we possess even after twenty centuries of Christian experience and reflection."

? Questions for Reflection

1. What threats do modern North American life and culture pose for the unity of the church? How does the "world" seek to achieve and maintain unity? What is distinctive about the Christian way of

understanding, achieving, and maintaining unity? Is unity always a good thing? In what ways is unity important in the contemporary church?

2. Paul directs the Philippians' attention to the practical implications of the theology expressed in one of their hymns. Select some favorite hymns and consider the practical implications of the beliefs expressed in them.

3. What citizenship is evident as you interact in the world? What mindset is evidenced by how the members of your church and/or denomination interact with one another?

4. How would our daily lives be different if we were to model our living after the Christ Hymn in Philippians 2:6–11? In what ways do we resist following the self-emptying model of Jesus? Is there a difference between humility and self-deprecation? How can we reclaim the image of servant or slave in the context of the history of oppression of women, the poor, and people of color?

The Worth of Our Résumés

The hymn Paul recites in 2:6–11 both tells the story of our salvation and offers a model of the life we are called to follow. At the end of chapter 2, Paul turns apparently to a new topic, travel plans for Timothy (2:19–24) and Epaphroditus (2:25–30), but in both cases he describes these coworkers in terms that make clear that he sees them, too, as models of life in Christ. Now, here in the third chapter, Paul will add his own life to the list of models for the Philippians to copy. As he says in 3:17, "Brothers and sisters, join in imitating me, and observe those who live according to the example you have in us."

The Imitation of Christ

Just as many modern readers are troubled by Paul's seemingly self-deprecating tone when he describes his relationship with Jesus Christ, many others may be troubled by the boastfulness and arrogance that sometimes seems to pervade Paul's self-expression. His frequent calls to "imitate me" and his talk of "boasting" ring in our ears as conceit. Here again, however, we are dealing with cultural differences. As one historian has put it, Roman culture was focused on the love of status and honor (MacMullen, 88–120, 125; see also Malina, *World*, 28–62). Those things in which one boasted—wealth, family status, a good name, pure ethnic bloodlines, for example—

> "In the first-century Mediterranean world, every social interaction that takes place outside one's family or outside one's circle of friends is perceived as a challenge to honor, a mutual attempt to acquire honor from one's social equal."—Bruce J. Malina, *The New Testament World*, third edition, 37.

were what constituted one's sense of honor. Boasting (1:26, 3:3), in other words, has to do with those things in which we place our pride and that tell us how we stand in relation to those around us. Second, when Paul, the slave of Christ Jesus, says, "Imitate me," he could just as well be saying "Imitate Christ," for that is whom he is imitating. His boasting and his calls to imitate are focused on Christ rather than on his own accomplishments (1:26). Just as Paul's apparent self-denial is what one would expect of an ancient Mediterranean slave in relation to the master, so also his talk of boasting and his willingness to hold his own life up for imitation were no cause for offense among people of Paul's day.

> "I want to know Christ and the power of his resurrection and the sharing of his sufferings by becoming like him in his death, if somehow I may attain the resurrection from the dead. Not that I have already obtained this or have already reached the goal; but I press on to make it my own, because Christ Jesus has made me his own."—Phil. 3:10–12

The same cannot be said, however, for the focus of his boasting and the ultimate object of his imitation, Christ Jesus, whose death on the cross symbolized the very opposite of honor. As Paul puts it in 1 Cor. 1:23, the proclamation of a crucified Christ was a stumbling block to Jews, who did not anticipate that the Messiah would so die, and foolishness to Greeks (i.e., non-Jews), for whom the idea of worshipping as Lord of all Creation a slave who had died on a cross would have sounded like complete lunacy. Yet that is precisely the message of the Christ Hymn and precisely what Paul announced as good news over and over again in his letters and, undoubtedly, in his sermons as he traveled around the empire.

Paul had to repeat this message so often because it was so thoroughly countercultural. Perhaps that's why he tells the Philippians that it's really no trouble for him "to write the same things" to them. After all, to do so is a "safeguard" for them (3:1b). He then proceeds to a discussion of circumcision that seems on the face of it to be a brand-new topic, introduced in an assertive tone that sounds jarring against what has preceded. The change of tone and topic is so abrupt, in fact, that many scholars regard this whole section (3:1b–ca. 4:3) as a portion of a separate letter, inserted here by a later editor. Much of the language in this section, however, is consistent with what we find in the preceding sections of the letter, especially in the Christ Hymn. However one decides this issue, the thematic coherence between this unit and the rest of the letter should not be overlooked.

Phil. 3:2–6: Confidence in the Flesh versus Boasting in Christ

If Paul has been attempting up to this point to secure the unity and partnership of the Philippian Christians against both external threats and internal dissensions, the discussion of circumcision is not out of place. We know from other letters of Paul, especially Galatians, that he regarded the imposition of circumcision on his Gentile converts as a fundamental threat to the gospel he preached. Paul sees circumcision as a form of putting "confidence in the flesh" (3:3–4), that is,

> "Beware of the dogs, beware of the evil workers, beware of those who mutilate the flesh!"—Phil. 3:2

as an element among the worldly credentials one accumulates in order to establish one's own honor or "righteousness" before God.

While the language with which Paul begins this discussion is usually translated as a strong warning—"Beware of the dogs, beware of the evil workers, beware of those who mutilate the flesh!" (3:2)—the verb (which means "to see" or "look at" something) is not accompanied by the grammatical cues that usually signal warning (Stowers, 116). Paul may be calling on the Philippians "to consider" or "examine" the example he now presents, which represents a sharp contrast with the examples of Christ, Timothy, and Epaphroditus that have preceded, and his own example, which follows. In any case, Paul's choice of terms to designate these opponents is derogatory, to say the least. Dogs were regarded as scavengers and were considered "unclean" among Jews. The term "dogs" was also used among Jews to designate Gentiles, which makes its use ironic here, where Paul is speaking of people who (whether Jews or Gentiles) were seeking to have Gentile Christians take up an elemental expression of Jewish identity. For Paul, such people are not only like (Gentile) dogs, but "evil workers" and "mutilators of the flesh." This last phrase translates a single Greek word, *katatome* ("mutilators," or "the mutilation"), a parody of the word for circumcision (*peritome*), which was a term of honor among many Jews of the day (Craddock, 56). Paul is not speaking here of the Jewish practice of circumcision, however, but specifically of Christians, whether Jews or Gentiles, who advocate circumcision of Gentile followers of Christ.

The acid in Paul's language might have shocked the Philippians even more than it does many of us. Jewish custom required circumcision not only of Jewish males, but of all serious Gentile proselytes, for as the mark of the covenant with Abraham (Gen. 17), it symbolized full identification with the people of Israel. The earliest Christians regarded themselves as a faithful expression (or extension) of Israel. Circumcision would thus have seemed to most Christian Jews, and not a few Gentile converts, an obvious step to take, for it would have signified the completion of their "adoption" as children of God. Like a parent warning children of the danger if they should slip from the bank into a stream, the edge in Paul's language functions as a sharp warning, meant to force their attention to the dangers of a practice that otherwise appears quite innocent. But what is it about circumcision that so threatens Paul? Why does he reckon it as "putting confidence in the flesh" rather than as an act of covenant faithfulness?

Both here and in Galatians (cf. 3:2, 5:5), Paul contrasts circumcision with "Spirit" and faith (Phil. 3:3, 9). The Spirit is the manifestation of God's grace-filled presence, made present now for all through Jesus' trust (faith) in God's promise. If the Spirit of God is already present, the logic seems to go, what more is needed? To use a crass analogy, if you've already been given title to the Mercedes, free and clear, why would you want to start making payments again? The answer might have to do with a need for security, the desire to do just a little more or to make sure that all the i's are dotted and the t's are crossed. But in doing so, one enters into a game that is difficult to stop, for the fundamental issue—trust or faith in God's graciousness—is not likely to be resolved by anything we do. Moreover, as we add each new item to the list of securities over which we exercise control, we mark new distinctions between ourselves and those around us, who have done a little more or a little less, or who have a different list of securities altogether. Rather than embodying God's oneness and standing together in one Spirit (1:27), we find ourselves marking differences, attending to our own interests, and dissembling into factions.

In short, while circumcision may strike our modern ears as a religious problem peculiar to Paul's culture, in fact it represents a nearly universal human problem, albeit one that takes different forms in different cultures. What is it, day in and day out, that we put our confidence and trust in? What do we have (or lack) that makes us feel better (or worse) than others around us? An ideal family? A nice house in the suburbs? A respected career? A Ph.D.? Material possessions? The right denominational affiliation? There may be nothing intrinsically wrong with any of these things, but when they come to represent marks of distinction and achievement in our own eyes they belie the genuineness of our faith in God's grace as shown in Jesus Christ. As Paul notes of circumcision in Galatians 5:6: "In Christ Jesus neither circumcision nor uncircumcision counts for anything; the only thing that counts is faith working through love."

In Phil. 3:3 Paul makes the provocative claim that worship in the Spirit of God, boasting in Christ Jesus, and putting no confidence in the flesh represent the "true circumcision." Yet he also wants to make clear that it is not because he himself has no grounds for boasting that he so readily dismisses whatever would constitute grounds for "confidence in the flesh." In essence, he says, "Look, it's not as though I couldn't play the game if I wanted to. In fact I can play it even better than anyone else" (3:4). He then proceeds to list the factors that, by the standards of a male, Hellenistic Jew of the first century, would have made a very impressive résumé (3:5–6).

With no little irony, he begins by noting that he was himself circumcised on the eighth day (literally, "as to circumcision, an eighth-dayer"), that is, the right day. He notes also that he is a full member of Israel, neither a convert nor the child of proselytes; in other words, his bloodlines are pure, a matter of great importance among Jews after the return from exile. He is a member specifically of the tribe of Benjamin, the last-born son of Jacob and Rachel. Benjamin was Joseph's only full brother and the only son of Jacob born in the Promised Land. Benjamin was the tribe from which came Israel's first king, Saul. Jerusalem lies within the borders of the land first given to this tribe. To claim membership in this tribe was a matter of some esteem and privilege among Jews of Paul's day. "Hebrew born of Hebrews" may again refer to the purity of his ancestry, but may also suggest that his family spoke Hebrew or Aramaic in their home (Craddock, 57)—Greek was more typical of Jews living away from Israel—and that they resisted Hellenizing cultural influences.

 Want to Know More?

About honor and status in first-century Rome? See Bruce J. Malina, *The New Testament World*, third edition (Louisville, Ky.: Westminster John Knox Press, 2001), chapters 1, 3.

About circumcision? See Paul J. Achtemeier, ed., *HarperCollins Bible Dictionary*, rev. ed. (San Francisco: HarperCollins, 1996), p. 185–86.

Paul had control over none of the factors he has mentioned thus far; they constituted the portions of his honor that were his by family. The next three items, however, designate matters over which Paul had control: he was a Pharisee, a persecutor of the church, and blameless with regard to the Law. While the Gospels portray some Pharisees as enemies of Jesus, they were held in esteem in their day because of their focus on matters of purity and table fellowship in their quest to live in holiness under the Law. Paul's esteem for the Law is also demonstrated clearly in his attacks upon the church prior to his calling in Christ Jesus (cf. Acts 7:58, 8:1, 9:1–2, Galatians 1:13–14, 23). Finally, Paul mentions his sense of righteousness: he is blameless as to what the Law requires. There is nothing ironic here in Paul's tone, nor any reason to think that he was deluding himself. His claim of "blamelessness" probably does not mean, however, that he thought he had never sinned. More likely, when he did fall short he made appropriate use of the Law's own prescriptions for restoration. Thus, the Law held no outstanding complaints against him. In any case, he claims his blameless righteousness with all integrity and sincerity. An impressive résumé indeed, both with regard to pedigree and accomplishment! If anyone among those who claim allegiance to Israel has the right to make the claim that he is a person of honor in the eyes of his peers and before God, it is Paul.

Phil. 3:7–16: Paul's New Résumé

In the repetitive statements (3:7–9) that follow this résumé, Paul emphasizes his complete detachment from this means of establishing his honor and status. Rather than using this résumé to certify his honor, he reckons all these things as "loss" (3:7, 8). Some translations obscure this nuance by using the expression "I have suffered the loss of all things," in verse 8 (Craddock, 59), thereby conveying a sense of passive regret at all of the good things that have been taken away from him, as if Paul were comparing himself here to Job. But this is not a lament. Paul is stressing what he has voluntarily renounced for the sake of gaining Christ, whose surpassing worth he now celebrates.

> "Paul does not toss away junk to gain Christ; he tosses away that which was of tremendous value to him. Therein lies the extraordinary impact of his testimony and the high commendation of faith in Jesus Christ."—Fred B. Craddock, *Philippians*, Interpretation, 58.

Paul now regards what he once cherished as *skubala*. Words commonly used in English translations for the Greek word are "excrement," "refuse," "dung," and "rubbish." These all fail, for the sake of polite speech, to catch the full force of the word. Paul is not trying to be polite; he's making an emphatic point by the use of repetition and strong, even offensive, words. We ought not to infer, however, that he had misjudged the intrinsic merit of the elements in his résumé, nor that these qualifications were bad, *in and of themselves.* The point is that in light of the surpassing worth of knowing Christ, what Paul once esteemed he now regards as worthless and as potential impediments, because they functioned as a false security for him and because they hindered his perception of the nature of God's righteousness, made known in Christ.

We need to be clear about what Paul is and is not contrasting. Paul is not deprecating Judaism, nor contrasting Judaism and Christianity as religious systems. Nor is he saying that the Law is worthless. He is describing the tendency of people in both traditions to "keep score" and, by that means, to mark distinctions between the righteous and the unrighteous. The fresh disclosure of God's righteousness and grace, made known to Paul by the crucified one, renders all scorekeeping useless at best (Meyer, 70). The contrast, then, is between Paul's values, focus, and means of defining his identity prior to and following his revelatory encounter with Christ.

> "Please understand, says Paul, I am not attacking the Jews. The point is, salvation does not rest with us but with God. . . . Religious pride is not the monopoly of the Jews. For Paul it was not the law but the law moved to the center as the ground of human righteousness which caused him to yell 'Beware!' "—Fred B. Craddock, *Philippians,* Interpretation, 55.

The contrasts continue in 3:9, focusing on righteousness. This word has lost most of its meaning except as a specialized religious and theological term. We do not have a word in English, in fact, that matches quite what the Greek conveys, though by using a combination of terms such as "right relationship," "justice," or "solidarity" we may get closer. The term designates what we hope for in the best of our relationships—trust, compassion, assurance that another will be with us, no matter what. When Paul speaks of "a righteousness of my own that comes from the law," he has in mind the relationship he once sought, on his own terms and based in the law—a relationship that he would merit and thus control. In contrast to this, he now talks of the righteousness of God that comes by faith, specifically by faith in Christ. The difference consists both in source and

> "His goal is clear: to be with Christ in the resurrection. To that end he can seek, because he has been found; he can know because he has been known; he can apprehend because he has been apprehended."—Fred B. Craddock, *Philippians,* Interpretation, 61.

29

nature. The kind of relationship with God that Paul now celebrates is rooted not in what Paul must do, but in his assurance that God is trustworthy and certain, as Jesus' trust in God and trustworthiness has demonstrated. Paul's faith, in turn, follows the same model. Because he trusts the God he knows in Jesus Christ, he wants to be like him—knowing both "the power of his resurrection" (power that vanquishes death) and, strikingly, the "sharing of his sufferings by becoming like him in his death." Here Paul reintroduces key terms from earlier in the letter. The members of verses 10 and 11 form an inverted parallelism: a) resurrection, b) suffering, b[1]) death, a[1]) resurrection. This structure joins these elements as an indivisible whole, just as in the two movements of the Christ Hymn (2:6–11).

In the following paragraph (3:12–16), Paul develops the (ever popular) image of a runner straining toward the finish line, an image that was familiar to people in Roman colonies like Philippi. With every ounce of energy focused upon that single goal, and "forgetting what lies behind," the distractions of prior accomplishments and any need for comparison with others fall to the side. "The heavenly call of God in Christ Jesus" (3:14), the only goal worth pursuing, focuses the whole of life, for both the individual and the community. As with the call to "work out your own salvation" in 2:12, Paul understands this activity not as his own doing but as what is now possible in Christ (3:12). The conversion of his imagination sets him free to work and to run without watching his feet. Though Paul uses the language of "maturity" or "perfection" (3:15), this is not a race for self-improvement. Those who are mature, who have the "same mind" (of Christ, cf. 2:5–11), run in freedom, joy, and partnership toward the one they trust.

> "Faith for him involved running, wrestling, striving, and fighting, none of which would end until the day of Christ. We must remember that for Paul all that effort was not for merit but was rather the activity of one who had abandoned all claim to merit."—Fred B. Craddock, *Philippians*, Interpretation, 61.

? Questions for Reflection

1. Who were the Judaizers? What was the significance of circumcision for them? How does Paul reinterpret "circumcision"? Where does the problem lie?
2. What things about yourself bring you the greatest sense of confi-

dence in your Christianity? What about yourself would you most want to hold up before God or other people as evidence of your faithfulness? What words could be used to replace "circumcision" in the Christian church, i.e., what rituals or actions do we rely on as evidence of our righteousness?

3. On what grounds do North Americans often establish a sense of personal security or status? What are the means by which we express our sense of status and self-worth publicly? How do such concerns affect our relationships with Christ? With others? -

4. What do you make of Paul's claim that he now boasts in Christ alone, rather than in those elements in which he once placed the greatest pride? What might it mean for us today—especially for our relationships—to put our confidence in Christ rather than in our own merits?

5. What is Paul's attitude toward his Jewish heritage? How do you reconcile Paul's humility with his "boasting" and setting himself up as an example?

3. wealth
   tech
   freedoms

Philippians 4:4–20

Participation with Paul in the Mission of God's Grace

In the last two chapters of his letter to the Philippians, Paul twice issues a command that has the sound of a refrain: "Finally, my brothers and sisters, rejoice in the Lord" (3:1); "Rejoice in the Lord always; again I will say, Rejoice" (4:4). These commands set the tone for the last chapter of the letter. While Paul may have concerns about aspects of the Philippians' circumstances, or his own, his admonition to joy offers the Philippians a model of one who presses on toward the goal, regardless of the situation, deeply enveloped in a sense of God's graceful presence.

Paul

Phil. 4:4–7: The Peace of God versus the Peace of Rome

Having begun the fourth chapter by urging unity between two women in the congregation, Euodia and Syntyche (4:2–3), he follows the call to rejoice (4:4) (or bids them farewell, Craddock, 41) with a brief series of general commandments and reassurances for the congregation as a whole. Each of these adds something to the picture of the mark toward which Paul and the Philippians press, as well as to the perspective he wants to see in them as they deal with whatever life brings them. The call to make their "gentleness" known to all (4:5) carries with it the sense that as they work with others around them, the patience and sustained openness they display has consequences for their mission, that is, their continuing proclamation and embodiment of God's good news in Jesus Christ, discerned most clearly in their unity (cf. 1:27, 2:1–3ff) and their suffering like Christ.

A reassurance follows the command to gentleness: "The Lord is near." This statement is often heard in temporal terms, that is, as indicating that he is coming back soon. While this is likely one aspect of this reference, as Paul never relinquished his expectation of the imminent return of Christ (Craddock, 71), it may also be understood spatially: in everything the church does in his name, Christ is "at hand" or present. The occasions on which this passage is scheduled as a lectionary reading—during the season of Pentecost (Jesus is present in the Spirit) and prior to Advent (we await his coming)—suggest the church adopted both senses (Craddock, 71). The paradox implied in these two senses may cause us more discomfort than it would have the Philippians.

> "One has to wonder how the church reacted to this response to their gift. Needless to say, commentators have been somewhat puzzled by it. Descriptions of 4:10–20 have included terms such as tense, detached, awkward, distant, and discourteous. The most generous comment spoke of the passage as evidence of Paul's being human."—Fred B. Craddock, *Philippians*, Interpretation, 76.

"Do not worry about anything" follows the statement about Jesus' nearness. Paul then tells the Philippians to pray—including both thanksgiving and requests (4:6). Perhaps the juxtaposition of prayer and presence arises in Paul's mind from his familiarity with the Psalms: "The Lord is near to all who call on him" (Psalm 145:18–19, cf. 34:17–18; 119:151) (Witherington, 112). Rejoicing, practicing gentleness, not worrying, praying with thanksgiving—together these suggest that Paul wants the Philippians to engage their context fully, but with perspectives transformed by their awareness of God's grace and presence.

This is borne out in 4:7, where Paul offers yet another reassurance: "And the peace of God, which surpasses all understanding, will guard your hearts and your minds in Christ Jesus." Peace is found not in circumstances, whether internal (dissensions) or external (opposition), but in God. Most striking, even ironic, is that Paul uses a military metaphor, "guard" or "stand sentry." Here again it is appropriate to remember the context in Philippi, a Roman military colony, as well as Paul's current circumstances as a Roman prisoner. But Paul may not be using this imagery simply because his and their circumstances suggest it. Remember, the phrase with which the verse begins contains an implicit claim that would have rung provocatively both in his prison cell and in Philippi, where Pax Romana (the "Peace of Rome"—social order through Roman domination) was the order of the day. Peace is not the gift of Caesar, Paul says, but the gift of God, and God's peace surpasses all our human understanding. If Paul and the Philippians trust God as the source of genuine peace, then they can surely also trust God to stand guard over their hearts and minds. Whatever the circumstances might suggest, there is no cause for worry, for God's peace—which has overcome even the power of death—reigns supreme. This reassurance is echoed in verse 9, following Paul's call to continue to study ("consider," "carefully evaluate") the virtues held up in Greek culture at large, while also following what they have seen in Paul. Throughout his farewell, then, we see Paul advocating not withdrawal from the world, but critical engagement with the world in both thought and practice, following Christ's model and relying on the peace of God that transcends circumstances.

Phil. 4:8–11: Friendship in Christ and the Sharing of Financial Resources

Paul now turns to a new topic, the Philippians' ongoing friendship with and care for Paul, demonstrated in their sharing of financial resources with him. This is the last major section of the letter, an odd place, it has seemed to many, to finally thank the Philippians for their financial support. Moreover, it seems to modern ears that Paul's "thank you" is virtually "thankless." Paul expresses his gratitude that "at last" they "have revived" their concern (4:10), as if he had been waiting impatiently for them to act. But then, it seems, he really didn't need it anyway, for he has learned to be content in all circumstances (4:11–13). Later he notes that it is really they who profit from this gift giving and offers them an official-sounding "paid in full" (4:17–18). Is this a genuine "thank you" after all and, if so, how heartfelt is it (Craddock, 76–77; Bockmuehl, 256–58)?

Most of the problems modern readers have with this passage stem once again from cultural differences and from our tendency to introduce our own expectations into the interpretation. We know what a "thank you" is supposed to sound like, and this doesn't sound to us like a very honest one. In this instance, however, what may seem on the surface to be the case is, in fact, something quite different. We need to recall, first of all, that Paul has been giving thanks for the Philippians' friendship and sharing with him in the gospel, including the suffering that comes with the ministry of the gospel, since the opening verses of the letter (1:3–11). Paul is grateful not only for the financial support the Philippians have shared, but also for their sharing and partnership in all aspects of his mission. The whole letter, in other words, is an extended, heartfelt "thank you."

We should also take note of the language of gratitude that permeates this section of the letter. This is the portion of a letter when ancient people would usually anticipate a message that would nurture strong positive feelings (Witherington, 122), and Paul does not disappoint here. Paul begins the section in verse 10 by using the language of joy ("I rejoice" or "I rejoiced") and later affirms their distinctive and continual sharing in the financial aspects of his mission (4:15–16). Finally, Paul describes their gifts as a "fragrant offering, a sacrifice acceptable and pleasing to God" (4:18). This is hardly faint praise. Nor does "at last you have revived your concern for me" necessarily denote impatience on Paul's part. As a traveling missionary in the world of the first century, and now as a prisoner of Rome, Paul was probably not the easiest person to stay in touch with. As he himself takes note, for a while they apparently "had no opportunity" to show their concern (4:10).

What about the sense Paul conveys that he didn't really need their gift (4:11–13)? We know from Paul's other letters that he takes pride in his self-sufficiency (cf. especially 1 Cor. 9), so we should not be too surprised to see the same attitude expressed here. This was not merely a matter of Paul's rugged individualism and

> "It seems as though the apostle realizes that he has spoken so much of the opposition and conflict between the culture and the church that points of commendation and agreement have been overlooked. In 4:8–9 he remedies that somewhat by commending to the Philippians a list of admirable traits drawn from Greek moralists: the true, the honorable, the just, the pure, the lovely, the excellent, the praiseworthy. These were the virtues extolled by the ethicists of Greek culture."—Fred B. Craddock, *Philippians*, Interpretation, 72–73.

> "In the final analysis, the God who 'is at work in you, both to will and to work for his good pleasure' (2:15) speaks the concluding word of approval or disapproval over all human behavior."—Fred B. Craddock, *Philippians*, Interpretation, 74.

> "Rejoice in the Lord always; again I will say, Rejoice. Let your gentleness be known to everyone. The Lord is near."—Phil. 4:4–5.

independence, as members of our culture might hear it. The cultural norms and economic patterns of the Roman Empire focused a great deal of attention on the reciprocal exchange of gifts and services. The opulence of gifts given to others was an expression both of one's own honor and the honor of the one on whom the gifts were bestowed. One gave gifts especially to those from whom one could expect some kind of return, whether it be in the form of services provided by a client for a patron or in opportunities for social or economic advancement. Some have compared the economy of the ancient world to a giant pyramid scheme, with people at each tier attempting to preserve their place, or possibly grease their way up the pyramid, by means of their benevolence toward those in adjacent tiers.

In the "patronage"-based economy of the Roman Empire, gifts were rarely given freely; they nearly always carried with them an expectation of some form of reciprocation, as gifts often do today (Malina, *World*, 99f.; "Patron and Client," 143–75). In contrast, Paul stresses throughout his letters that God's grace is something given freely, an expression of God's essential graciousness and mercy, and without the expectation that some service or offering must be performed in return. This image of God's grace challenges those who follow in the way of Christ to reformulate all of their relationships around the principle of grace, rather than continue in the same tradition of reciprocal demand and expectation that had marked their relationships until they met Christ. Thus, Paul is thankful not only for the gift they have given him, but also for the fact that it expresses their continuing participation in this wholly new way of constructing relationships—the partnership they have in Christ.

Phil. 4:12–13: Security and Partnership in Christ

The way God's grace transforms the social and economic arenas of life may shape our understanding of Paul's thinking in this passage in at least two ways. First, he tells the Philippians that he has learned to deal with his circumstances whether he has plenty or only a little, whether he is hungry or well fed (4:12). Paul's apparent self-sufficiency should be understood as an expression of his dependence on God for all that he needs (4:13). In verse 12 he uses an expression heard commonly in one of the popular religious genres of his day: "I have learned the secret . . ." In other words, he presents his capacity to adjust to his circumstances as if it were insight granted to him as a divine revelation. We might then be warranted in reading 4:13 as his attempt to put this insight into words, i.e., "The secret is: I can do all things through the one who strengthens me." He didn't really need their gift, in other words, because he is adept at adapting, secure in his certainty that it is God who strengthens him. This is not a statement of self-sufficiency, then, as much as it expresses his complete trust and sense of sufficiency in God. As members of a deeply materialistic culture, we might ask how many of us could or would make the same claim.

Second, his apparent self-sufficiency (which is actually his reliance on God) also serves as part of his attempt to steer clear of the sense of obligation that attends gift giving and structures relationships—preserving an imbalanced, hierarchical economy—in his cultural context (cf. also 1 Cor. 9:12b ff., 2 Cor. 12:13, 1 Thess. 2:9) (Witherington, 123–26; Perkins, 100–01). As he says in Romans 13:8, his goal is that Christians should "owe no one anything, except to love one another." As long as the suspicion of obligation attends our sharing with one another, we will never experience whatever we share as an expression of genuine love. In other words, he shapes his own ministry and wants to shape the ministry of his congregations in such a way that it is clear that the gifts they share with one another are given in love (i.e., rooted in God's love for us) rather than from any sense of obligation. Given the way the culture and economy of Paul's day were shaped around the obligatory exchange of gifts, Paul's practice would have represented both a foundational threat to the existing order of things and an opportunity—for most people the only opportunity they would ever have—to learn the experience of real freedom.

> "Perhaps Paul does feel some inner conflict between the need to express pleasure over the gift and at the same time witness to his freedom from the victimizing power of material things. . . . It is therefore important, perhaps even necessary, for Paul to state again his freedom, to relate the gift to ministry . . . and to God . . . and not to himself personally. In other words, the intimacy of giving and receiving must be balanced with distance, discourteous as it may sound."—Fred B. Craddock, *Philippians*, Interpretation, 77–78.

Phil. 4:14–20: Partnership in Christ and a Life of Integrity

After all of Paul's discussion of his dependence on God and not really needing their gift, Paul apparently shifts direction in verses 14–20. He says that what the Philippians did by becoming "co-partners" or "co-sharers" (the same word used in 1:7, "for all of you share in God's grace with me") in his "distress" or "affliction" is nonetheless good (4:14). He adds, in essence, that they are the exception that proves the rule: no other congregation partnered with him as they did in "the matter of giving and receiving" (4:15), language that suggests this "matter" was a topic of some concern and care on Paul's part. They are not only the exceptions, they are exceptional, too. Even before he left Macedonia, while he was in Thessalonica, they sent help more than once (4:16). He thus praises them for their caring and generous participation in God's grace in this way. The relationship he has with them is not that of typical patrons and clients, not a relationship of obligation, but a relationship of grace.

As he again makes clear, his primary interest is not in the gifts themselves, but in "the profit that accumulates to your account" (4:17). The language here may be both metaphorical and concrete. He may indeed have had something like "an account" with them, which has now been paid in full and more (4:18). This is language at home in the world of commerce (Craddock, 76; Osiek, 121f.).

Want to Know More?

About exchanging of gifts in the Roman Empire? See Bruce J. Malina, *The New Testament World,* third edition (Louisville, Ky.: Westminster John Knox Press, 2001), p. 99f.

Metaphorically, the "account" may refer to their standing before God; by participating with Paul in their gracious way, the Philippian Christians have fully demonstrated their participation not only in his ministry but, more important, in God's grace-filled way in the world. Now Paul shifts to the language of worship (Craddock, 76): the gifts he has received from their emissary Epaphroditus (or perhaps his presence is the "gift") are a "fragrant offering, a sacrifice acceptable and pleasing to God" (4:18). The certainty of this relationship allows Paul to affirm that God will fully satisfy all of their needs. The modifier "according to God's riches in glory in Christ Jesus" specifies the terms of this fulfillment. Paul is thinking not merely of physical satisfaction of needs, but of the kind of honor (glory) that is theirs in Christ Jesus, the crucified Messiah whose own humiliation, obedience, and death establish the model for their life together. Fittingly, the passage closes on a note of doxology; worship and praise of God are the focus of Christian life, and the tones with which the letter begins (1:11) and ends.

Regardless of whether one reads the words of 4:15–18 literally or metaphorically, the use of the language of commerce beside the language of liturgy demonstrates the integration in Paul's thought of aspects of existence that we customarily keep separate (Craddock, 78–79). Indeed, in Paul's day, people did not ordinarily distinguish such matters as religion, politics, economics, and family life. The "household" incorporated all of these dimensions of human experience within a single entity. Our more "atomized" approach to understanding our lives would have been impossible for someone like Paul to imagine. Thus, worshipping the God of Jesus Christ, sharing/partnering in the ministry of grace, and living within the Roman Empire as a people with citizenship elsewhere (3:20) are fully integrated with one another. Everything in Paul's experience and thought is now rooted firmly within the framework of the gospel he proclaims. All meaning in his life is determined through his experience in Christ Jesus. The integrity of his faith convictions and experience—which he also presumes of the Philippians—ought to challenge us to examine the ways we have grown comfortable with more compartmentalized approaches to life. Some would suggest that it is this very compartmentalization that allows the compromises we make between our faith and the culture in which we live. The letter to the Philippians challenges readers, not only here, but throughout, to reconsider some of our most basic assumptions about the gospel and the life of grace we share with God and God's people.

? Questions for Reflection

1. What might Paul mean when he says, "The Lord is near" (4:5)? How do we experience the nearness of the Lord? Historically it has been difficult for churches to keep the "already, but not yet" nature of Christ's presence in balance. Consider the different churches in your area: Are there those who focus almost entirely on the future coming of Christ and others who focus on the presence of Christ in the church with no sense of anticipation? Where does your community fall in this continuum?

2. In this last chapter of Philippians, Paul stresses peace and rejoicing, themes that he has developed earlier in the letter. What is the relationship between the circumstances of life and joy? By what means do we secure peace, whether personal or communal? To what extent are joy and peace related to our sense of the nearness

of Christ (cf. 4:4–7)? How do these definitions compare with our culture's understanding of joy and peace?

3. In his thanksgiving to the Philippians, Paul seems to teeter between gratitude and independence. How does this relate to the common understanding of giving in Roman society? How does it compare to the common understanding of giving in our society?

4. In Philippians 4:17–20, Paul uses both commercial and liturgical terms to describe his relationship with the Philippians, reflecting his understanding that all aspects of who a person is are integrated and that faith affects the entire person. In what ways does our compartmentalization of the self (my financial life, my vocational life, my family life, my national citizenship, my spiritual life . . .) keep us from faithfulness? Are there aspects of life that are considered "off limits" in your church? How valid is this?

5

Paul's Gospel under Threat

Paul's letter to the Galatians provides us with an immediate sense of the Apostle's passionate feelings for his congregations, as well as a powerful reminder of the world-shaking nature of the gospel. Here Paul takes to task a congregation that is at risk of leaving behind "the truth of the gospel" in favor of a more secure, if more traditional, form of religiosity. As he addresses this community and its concerns, his arguments take us to the heart of his understanding of the human condition before God since the

Galatia during Paul's travels

revelation of Jesus Christ, and thus not only to religious concerns, but to foundational questions about the way we shape our identities and order our relationships with one another. His insight into the significance and consequences of the "revelation of Jesus Christ" (1:12) for those who live in "the present evil age" (1:4) has given this letter a power in the Christian tradition that belies its relative brevity.

Gal. 1:1–2: Paul's Gospel Comes from God, Not from Humans!

As in Philippians and Paul's other letters, we find important hints about the tone and key issues of the letter to the Galatians in the first few verses. The "address" begins with Paul's most common self-designation, "Paul an apostle." But then, just where we might expect the simple referent "of Christ Jesus" (cf. 1 Cor. 1:1, 2 Cor. 1:1), Paul adds a modifying phrase found nowhere else in his letters: "sent neither by human commission nor from human authorities, but through (or "by") Jesus Christ and God the Father, who raised him from the dead" (1:1). The first part of this modifier denies human agency in Paul's apostleship. He has been sent on a mission (the meaning of "apostle") neither by a community nor by an individual. Paul will later clarify that this does not mean he is a renegade operating entirely on his own, for he has indeed consulted with the leaders of the Jerusalem church (1:18–19, 2:1–10), but that he owes his understanding of the gospel and his commissioning as an apostle to God alone, who has called him through (or "by") the revelation of Jesus Christ (1:12). Paul's need to confirm his call to mission as one of divine source and mediation suggests that opponents have challenged his authority in the Galatian church and questioned the sufficiency of the gospel he preaches. These concerns will occupy Paul's attention throughout the first two chapters of this letter. As the letter continues, however, it will become clearer that it is not Paul's own authority that is his primary concern, so much as the primacy, authenticity, and complete sufficiency of the good news he has proclaimed to them. Paul himself, in other words, is not the issue. The issue is the truth of the gospel.

After denying human agency in his mission, Paul identifies both Jesus Christ and "God the Father" as the true source of his mission. It is important to remember that the compound name "Jesus Christ" is actually a confession that Jesus is the Messiah of Israel and carries with it a twofold shock. First, for Paul the meaning of the term Messiah, or Christ, is now defined by the story of Jesus of Nazareth. Second, Israel's Messiah, the anointed one of prophetic hope, was crucified as a common criminal by Rome, at the instigation of Israel's leaders. "God the Father," the second title in this affirmation of divine agency, not only affirms the connections between Jesus, God, and Paul, but also prepares Paul's readers for the idea he will develop as the letter proceeds (1:3, 1:4, 3:7, 3:26, 4:2, 4:4–7, 4:22–31)—that the Galatian Christians are the children of God, adopted and set free by their gracious Father (Betz, 39 n. 27; Martyn, 84). For a Gentile audience such as the Galatians—who

> "I am astonished that you are so quickly deserting the one who called you in the grace of Christ and are turning to a different gospel—not that there is another gospel, but there are some who are confusing you and want to pervert the gospel of Christ."—Gal. 1:6–7.

probably regarded divine figures as dangerous powers needing to be appeased—the affirmation that the one true God of the universe was loving and merciful would have been a new concept, and one that required frequent confirmation. Furthermore, this is the God who raised Jesus from the dead, thereby overcoming all powers that enslave humankind, even death itself. By the resurrection God also confirms Jesus' messiahship and establishes him as Lord of the creation.

Finally, Paul completes the address by also naming as co-senders "all the members of God's family who are with me" (1:2). Here Paul affirms a familial relationship with God for all sisters and brothers in Christ. He then names those who are to receive this letter, the "churches in Galatia," but something is missing. Unlike the addresses of most of his other letters, Paul does not embed praise for the Galatians within his identification of them as the audience (e.g., "to all the saints in Christ Jesus who are in Philippi" [Phil. 1:1]; "to those who are sanctified in Christ Jesus, called to be saints" [1 Cor. 1:2]; "to all God's beloved in Rome, who are called to be saints" [Rom. 1:7]). The spare greeting of Galatians gives the letter a more brusque, formal tone and indicates the seriousness of the topic he is addressing (Martyn, 86). Second, Paul identifies the recipients as "churches of Galatia," indicating that the letter is sent not to one congregation, but many. This may not mean that the Galatian Christians were relatively numerous (see Stark, 3–27), but that they were members of a number of households in the region of Galatia. Scholars have long debated the precise meaning of the geo-graphical designation "Galatia," which traditionally referred to an area of northern, central Asia Minor, populated by Celts, with Ancyra, Pessinus, and Tavium as primary cities. Following Roman conquest, this region was expanded to include non-Celtic Pisidian Antioch, Lystra, and Derbe in southern, central Asia Minor, and the whole region was made a Roman province in 25 BCE. Paul's use of the term "Galatians" (from Gaul: Celts) as a form of direct address in 3:1 may suggest that he has in mind congregations in the northern part of the province, for there were probably few Celts living in the southern regions of the province. The issue makes little difference in the interpretation of the letter, except that it may help us to know a bit

---

Galatia

Galatia was a territory in northcentral Asia Minor that was dominated by the Gauls, a Celtic tribe, from the third to the first century BCE. It was also a Roman province after the first century BCE that included portions of other territories. There is debate among scholars as to exactly what area was meant by Galatia (or the variant, Gaul) in the New Testament.

---

more about the people to whom Paul writes and the kinds of issues they faced. In the northern areas of the province there was little or no Jewish presence. This means that Paul is probably not addressing household churches made up of a mixture of Jewish and Gentile members, as would be true in some of his other letters (e.g., Romans). The people Paul addresses in this letter were Gentiles who had worshipped pagan gods and who had not been circumcised.

Gal. 1:3–5: God Has Set Us Free from the Power of Sin

Following the address, the greeting proper is found in verses 3 and 4. It follows a fairly typical Pauline formula, announcing grace and peace from God, once again identified as "our Father," and "the Lord Jesus Christ." As noted in the discussion of Philippians, Paul's association of grace and peace with the God of Israel would have carried a confrontational ring given the dominance of the Empire's rhetoric of the "peace of Rome." The same is true of the confessional claim that Jesus Christ (rather than Caesar, or a member of the Roman pantheon) is Lord (see also 6:14, 18). More than just a greeting, then, these statements announce a reordering of worldviews. Verse 4 continues the greeting with a series of clauses modifying "the Lord Jesus Christ." Nowhere else in Paul's epistolary greetings do we find anything quite like the pronouncements found here, which move from confession to praise of God and thereby evoke the atmosphere of worship (Martyn, 87). Paul thus seems to invite the Galatians to join him in worship of God, to remember and re-embody the originating context and expression of their faith.

> "It is significant that nowhere in the beginning of this epistle does Paul express his gratitude for or make a word of affirmation about his readers . . . When believers are abandoning the gospel for a perversion of the truth, the situation leaves him little for which to be thankful. There is no reason to pretend that things are better than they are. The issue is frankly grave."—Charles B. Cousar, *Galatians*, Interpretation (Atlanta, John Knox Press, 1982), 19.

Paul begins with an early Christian confession: Jesus Christ is the one who "gave himself for our sins." His life was not taken from him; rather, he gave it freely in order to set us free from the claim and power our sins—both personal and corporate—have over us. Because we hear this phrase so often in the church, we may miss its provocation or, as our individualistically oriented culture has taught us, turn it into a matter of personal introspection. Paul understands sins, or sin (as he more often speaks of it), not as bad things we choose to do but as a "law" or corrupting force at work in the world, darkening our minds and imagination (see Romans 7:12–25) and prohibiting us from doing—or even knowing!—what is God's will. Thus, Paul often contrasts the realm or space where sin rules with the realm in which God's Spirit is the operating power. When we live in the realm of sin, we can no more choose not to sin than we can choose not to breathe. Thus, Paul's argument here addresses the sins of individuals not with offers of individual forgiveness, but with the pronouncement that sin's power has been swept aside.

The next clause, "to set us free from the present evil age," makes still clearer that Paul is not thinking of sins merely as individual actions for which we are responsible but as an occupying force from which we have been liberated. Here we also have the first hint of the ways Paul's thinking in this letter is shaped by the language and imagery of Jewish apocalyptic eschatology (Cousar, 17, 65). In this way of seeing reality, humankind has been and is held captive under the powers of "the present evil age." But now the power of God, which has entered the world in Jesus Christ, is overwhelming the corrupting power of sin (or "flesh" or "the world"), making it possible for humankind to join with and participate in the Christ-life. While Christians still await the full realization of God's redeeming presence in creation, Paul regards this redemption nonetheless as virtually an accomplished fact. This is the "grace"—the good news—of which Paul has already spoken in his greeting (1:3). For Paul, salvation thus means movement from one realm of power to another, and thus also from the experience of bondage to the experience of freedom. Paul in fact uses a verb here that means to "snatch from the grasp of" to indicate the fact that Christ's self-giving on the cross robs sin of its power to hold us captive.

If the Galatians were for some reason worried about the reality of their salvation, or tempted to pursue some additional security measures to protect themselves from further sins or to affirm their integral relationship with God's people, Paul is effectively reminding them that their salvation is already an

> "To suggest, then as the agitators at Galatia were doing, that Christ's death was insufficient and needed to be supplemented with further rites and rules was to advocate a position contrary to the will of God."— Charles B. Cousar, *Galatians*, Interpretation, 18.

accomplished reality. Thus, Paul does not call on the Galatians to "hold on tight" until salvation becomes a reality, or to pray that they are not tempted beyond their capacity to endure, but to remember that God has already completed their redemption in Jesus Christ, who gave himself for them on the cross. The only real threat to their salvation is the seduction to live as if it were not already accomplished, whether by giving practical allegiance to the Empire, for example, or even by seeking to secure their destiny through devoted religious practices. For Paul, the revelation of Christ means that all human traditions and social systems—including religious systems, whereby one seeks to be in positive relationship with the gods or God—are now rendered obsolete. One can say, in fact, that the central issue in Galatians is the revelation of Christ versus religion (Martyn, 37).

In the final modifying clause of verse 4, Paul adds that all of this redemptive activity in Jesus Christ was accomplished "according to the will of our God and Father"—the third time Paul has so named God in this greeting. Everything has taken place according to God's plan and, by implication, anything that others might suggest should be added to the picture of salvation would be a human construction and *contrary* to God's will. The greeting then comes to a fitting conclusion in the doxology of verse 5: "to whom be the glory forever and ever. Amen." The worship of God is the goal of human history and thus also an appropriate conclusion to a greeting that has focused on the grace of salvation in Christ. As the Creator, God stands beyond human perceptions and arrangements of time and space; "forever and ever" denotes not the endless duration of human time, but the story of God's grace that is beyond human reckoning.

> "To the people of Galatia there had come people saying that Paul was not really an apostle and that they need not listen to what he had to say. They based their belittlement on the fact that he had not been one of the original twelve, that, in fact, he had been the most savage of all persecutors of the Church, and that he held, as it were, no official appointment from the leaders of the Church. Paul's answer was not an argument; it was a statement. He owed his apostleship to no man but to a day on the Damascus Road when he had met Jesus Christ face to face. His office and his task had been given him direct from God."—William Barclay, *The Letters to the Galatians and the Ephesians*, rev. ed, Daily Study Bible, 7.

Gal. 1:6–10: A Rebuke in Place of a Thanksgiving

Galatians is the only letter in which Paul does not move from the address to a statement—usually a prayer—of thanksgiving for God's redeeming grace at work in the life of the congregation (see Philippians 1:3–10). The absence of a thanksgiving is yet another clue that Paul's relationship with the Galatians has deteriorated or is severely threatened. The rebuke (1:6–9) that here takes the place of a thanksgiving does serve a similar rhetorical purpose, however, in that it continues to emphasize the major theme of this letter. Paul describes the Galatians' turn toward the teaching of others as a "defection"—not from Paul but from God and from God's grace (1:6). Paul first describes this alternative teaching as a "different gospel," but then backtracks, for he knows that there is but one true gospel, only one message of God's grace in Christ (1:7). There are some, he says, who are confusing (or frightening) the Galatians and calling them aside toward a perverted version of the gospel (1:7). Paul avoids naming these persons explicitly, but it seems clear from the way Paul distinguishes "some," who are causing distress, from "you" (the plural pronoun refers to the Galatian Christians) that these opponents are teachers or evangelists from outside the congregation (see Cousar, 5–6). They may have been Christian Jews, like Paul himself, but advocates of a form of Christianity that retained traditional marks of Jewish culture, including circumcision and law keeping. Paul presents them in this letter as if they are introducing a Judean form of religion to the Galatians, with disastrous consequences for the Galatians' appropriation of the gospel of grace. The verb Paul uses here carries the sense of "troubling" or "causing anxiety and fear," not merely creating intellectual confusion.

Paul then offers a double curse upon any—whether humans, or angels, or even himself—who proclaims a version of the gospel that contradicts what they had first heard from him (1:8–9). It is not that he had the words just right at that time, but that there is nothing further to add, and no

> "The opponents in Galatia have either deliberately set out to undermine the authenticity of Paul's message by declaring his apostleship an inferior one, or, more likely, they have implied as much by the manner and content of their own preaching."—Charles B. Cousar, *Galatians*, Interpretation, 16.

The Outsiders

Many attempts have been made to name the itinerant missionaries who in Paul's absence had such an influence on the Galatians, the ones Paul referred to as agitators and troublemakers. Charles Cousar, in his Interpretation volume, lists five of the more important possibilities:

1. They were Jewish Christians from Jerusalem who claimed they had the support of James;
2. They were Jewish Christians, but with no support from the Jewish authorities in Jerusalem;
3. They were Jewish Christians of Gnostic persuasion, who did not care about the law and acted independently of the church;
4. They were not Jews but Gentile Christians who were loyal to the church leaders in Jerusalem;
5. They were composed of two groups: one a group of activists who urged submission to the law, the other a group of radicals who felt they were exempt from moral issues.

new requirements, if in fact God's redeeming grace has been made known and already experienced in Jesus Christ. In these verses of rebuke, Paul implicitly affirms the authority of the gospel as foundational to all of Christian experience. It is not himself, a doctrine, idea, or a book, nor even "Church" or "Scripture," that he here lifts up as authoritative so much as the life-altering authority of God's grace. The good news of Jesus Christ is the norm against which all other sermons or teachings, theologies or worldviews, and religious, economic, and cultural systems must be judged. God's grace in Christ Jesus "authors" and "authorizes" a new creation.

Want to Know More?

About Galatia and the Galatians? See Charles B. Cousar, *Galatians*, Interpretation (Atlanta: John Knox Press, 1982), 3–4; Paul J. Achtemeier, ed., *HarperCollins Bible Dictionary*, rev. ed. (San Francisco: HarperCollins, 1996), 357.

About the agitators? See Charles B. Cousar, *Galatians*, Interpretation (Atlanta: John Knox Press, 1982), 5–6; Calvin J. Roetzel, *The Letters of Paul: Conversations in Context*, fourth ed. (Louisville, Ky.: Westminster John Knox Press, 1998), 98–100.

About James? See Paul J. Achtemeier, ed., *HarperCollins Bible Dictionary*, rev. ed. (San Francisco: HarperCollins, 1996), 480.

In verse 10 Paul turns from his rebuke of the Galatians for deserting God to a series of rhetorical questions focusing on his own allegiance to God. His point, however, is not to focus attention on himself, but to establish clear alternatives in the Galatians' minds. He wants them to consider whether his actions— and their actions—are focused on "seeking human approval" or "God's approval." As he notes, if he were still seeking approval from human beings he would no longer be a slave of Jesus Christ. This contrast puts human honor and worldly success in stark relief against the location of one's identity in Christ; for Paul these are mutually exclusive alternatives. To be sure, by pleasing God one might also please human beings, especially in the church. But by focusing one's energies on pleasing humans, whose vision and values are mediated by "this present evil age," one will necessarily become a slave to the powers of the broken creation. Here again, as in the greeting (1:1–5) and rebuke (1:6–9), the central issue is the sufficiency of God's grace expressed in Christ's death for us: Does Christ set us free from the corrosive power of sin or not? Does God's grace in Christ offer the solution to destructive quests for human security and salvation or not? Is the cross of Christ the locus of redemption and grace or not? Is the source of our identity now rooted in Christ or not (Cousar, 19)?

"Am I now seeking human approval, or God's approval? Or am I trying to please people? If I were still pleasing people, I would not be a servant of Christ."—Gal. 1:10

48

? Questions for Reflection

1. How would you describe Paul's tone in this letter? To what do you attribute it? What is the significance of the intensity of Paul's reaction to the Galatian situation?
2. What is the nature of the teaching Paul's opponents have brought to the congregations in Galatia? What is so threatening about their teaching? What contemporary parallels do you see to the kind of teaching Paul's opponents are setting forth?
3. Paul continually makes the point that Christ is sufficient, that the grace of God transcends any religious system. This is a very difficult concept for people to grasp as is demonstrated by the fact that throughout history, Christians have fallen into the trap of adherence to religious systems as a means of justification. In what sense might it have been true that the revelation of Jesus Christ rendered Paul's own Jewish religiosity obsolete? What are the characteristics of contemporary Western "Christian religiosity"? Is it possible that taking seriously the "Christian faith"—at least a radical version like Paul's—would render obsolete our contemporary expressions of Christianity?
4. Summarize Paul's main message(s) in the letter to the Galatians in brief statements. How would it adjust our day-to-day "religious" focus were we to take seriously the message that "Christ is sufficient"? Is it possible that our focus on and arguments about rules and rituals serve us by allowing us to distract ourselves from the real business of God's claim upon our lives (e.g., challenging injustice, living in a fellowship that transcends national and cultural boundaries, seeking peace)?

6 | Galatians 1:11-2:10

The Power of the Gospel in Paul's Life

Once Paul finishes expressing his astonishment at the Galatians for their rapid desertion from God (1:6) and affirms that there is but one gospel (1:7–9), he turns to an extended account of his own call to the gospel and his relationship with the leaders of the church in Jerusalem. Within this section we learn more about Paul's career than we do in any other letter. But Paul's goal is not to talk about himself, nor even to defend his apostleship per se, even though a superficial reading could give this impression. Throughout, his focus is on the singularity of the gospel of grace in Christ Jesus and the unity of the church that has been called into being through the power of the gospel (Cousar, 26).

First Paul affirms that the gospel he has proclaimed came not through human agents but through a revelation of Jesus Christ (1:11–12). Although Paul has just issued a sharp rebuke to the Galatians, he now addresses them in familial tones ("brothers and sisters," 1:11). Although he is deeply frustrated with them, he continues to regard them as members of his family in Christ. Paul's assertion is that the gospel he preached neither originated with a person nor was passed on or taught to him by people. The gospel he proclaims is neither a human creation nor what people usually think of as "good news" (Martyn, 142, 146–48). Paul may have in mind not only the kind of news one might hear in the marketplace but the propagandistic claim of the Roman Empire to be the source of "good news." It further suggests that the gospel he preached did not come

> "You have heard, no doubt, of my earlier life in Judaism. I was violently persecuting the church of God and was trying to destroy it. I advanced in Judaism beyond many among my people of the same age, for I was far more zealous for the traditions of my ancestors."—Gal. 1:13–14

50

to him through a line of human agents as human tradition. Rather, he received this gospel by means of a revelation of Jesus Christ.

The gospel that Paul *experienced*—the power of God that breaks into life and changes people (and has changed Paul!)—is the real authority in Paul's life and the authority he is urging upon the Galatians (Cousar, 28). Paul supports this claim by describing his call (1:13–17). He then addresses the questions that might have arisen in the community regarding his visits (2:1–10). Finally, Paul describes a confrontation between Cephas (Peter) and himself that took place in Antioch (1:18–21), which will be the focus of the next unit. Each of these topics relates in some way to two central issues: the nature of the gospel and the unity of the church.

Gal. 1:13–17: Paul's Call

While some use the term "conversion" to designate the Damascus event in Paul's life, "call" is preferable for a number of reasons, not least of which because it is the term Paul himself uses (1:15) (Cousar, 33f.). "Call" also better incorporates the dual sense of conversion and commissioning, both of which are integral to this

Paul's conversion on the Damascus Road

account. "Conversion" often suggests to modern readers the sense of movement from evil to good, impious to pious, or from nonreligious to religious. In Paul's case, what we observe is a complete shift of focus and orientation as a result of the revelation of Jesus Christ. He was already, by his own accounts here and in Phil. 3:4–11, a person of surpassing piety, commitment, and zeal. Because of the revelation of Jesus Christ, he serves not a different God but the God he now perceives through the lens of his knowledge of Christ. As a consequence, it might be more accurate to describe his conversion as a shift from religious obsession focused on boundaries

> ### Revelation
>
> What did Paul mean when he said that he received the Gospel "through a revelation of Jesus Christ" (1:12)? Charles Cousar contends that Paul did not mean that he had received new information that no one else had (which is one possible interpretation), but that "the veil which has hidden God's Son from him is removed and Paul sees him." (Charles B. Cousar, *Galatians*, Interpretation, 28)

and purity to a vision of human freedom that transcends any religious system (Cousar, 36).

Changes

Charles Cousar notes two important changes in Paul that are dealt with in his letter to the Galatians:

1. Paul's new understanding of Christ. "One reason why Paul had reacted as vigorously as he did in opposition to the first Christians was their incomprehensible message about a crucified Messiah. . . . Such a message to a Jew is offensive—until one is grasped by that Christ and discovers that he has been established Son of God in power."

2. Paul's new view of the people of God. "As a Pharisee . . . it was outrageous to consider that the Messiah had been revealed to people who were at best religiously marginal, who lacked sufficient piety and commitment to the law, and who could be looked on with contempt. Paul's conviction was abruptly reversed, however, and he found himself engaged in a mission" to these Jews and also to Gentiles.

Paul hints at something of his critical attitude toward "religion" when he describes his earlier life in "Judaism" (1:13), a term that occurs in the New Testament only here and in the next verse, where he notes that he was advanced among his peers in the pursuit of this way of relating to God and totally devoted to the Jewish traditions. His devotion is also clear in his aggression against the "church of God"—both in violent persecution and his attempt to destroy it. Paul leaves little question about his hostility toward followers of Jesus. If those who are troubling the Galatians are suggesting that becoming a follower of Christ entails a subsequent step toward devotion to Jewish Law and culture, Paul knows otherwise. He can speak from experience to those who would require the Galatians to "Judaize" (cf. Gal. 2:14) as a part of their "Christizing." He was once very successful at just that kind of religiosity, but now he has been called to something fundamentally at odds with that pursuit—neither a better piety nor merely a different religion.

That transformation or conversion experience is the call of God, in grace, to both know Christ and to make Christ known. Paul's language may be intentionally ambiguous: the Greek of 1:16 can mean "to reveal God's son" either "to me" or "in me." Both ways of reading the phrase accurately describe dimensions of Paul's (and every Christian's) calling. Paul intentionally couches his description of this experience in language reminiscent of God's calls to the prophets Isaiah (Isa. 49:1–6) and Jeremiah (Jer. 1:4–5). Like both prophets, Paul has been called by God from his mother's womb. Like both prophets, his call also entails a proclamation to the nations. Like both prophets, Paul's call entails both faithfulness to God and a sharp break with the past. The proclamation of good news to the nations, in particular, was understood by Paul and others of his day as an expectation reserved for the last days, when God would not only restore Israel but transform the whole creation, gathering the remnants of the nations alongside Israel to worship God (Isa. 45:18–25).

In verses 16c–17, Paul turns again to the contrast between divine and human agency. When God was pleased—calling him from the womb and by grace—to reveal God's son to/in him, Paul did not "confer with any human being," not even with any of those in Jerusalem who had already been called as apostles before him. Instead he went to Arabia and then returned again to Damascus. Rather than seek confirmation or instruction from the leaders of the church in Jerusalem, Paul removes himself to an unknown location, away from physical settings of his former life, until he returns to the site of his call (Damascus). All of this functions as strong denial of any dependency of the gospel he preached on human tradition.

> "But what does it really mean to live as one so called and grasped? Two things at least are worth noting. First, it means that life has direction and purpose. . . . Secondly, the reality of being called and grasped provides enormous support for getting about one's task. . . . The decision as to what one is ultimately about in life, that is, being a Christian, is not one's own to be fretted over; it is God's decision. That takes a burden off and opens up incredible resources for coping with life and its problems."—Charles B. Cousar, *Galatians*, Interpretation, 32–33.

Gal. 1:18–2:10: Paul's Visits to Jerusalem

The Galatians probably know that Paul has made visits to Jerusalem. Perhaps they have heard of these visits from those who are now troubling them, who might have cited the visits as evidence that Paul's understanding of the gospel was not firsthand, but derived from the Jerusalem church, or that his gospel was a watered-down version of the full, original version of Christian life practiced and taught by the Jerusalem apostles. To counter any such notions, Paul describes his two visits to Jerusalem. The careful way in which Paul nuances these accounts and his strong assertion of his integrity—"before God, I do not lie" (1:20)—lend weight to the proposal that he is countering very specific attacks upon his status as an apostle and, thereby, the adequacy of the gospel he has preached.

The first time Paul went to Jerusalem, three years after his call (1:18–24), he says, he stayed a relatively brief time (fifteen days) with Cephas (Peter) and did not even see any other apostles except James. He carefully describes this as a "visit" (rather than a "meeting," for example). Then, he says, he went away into the regions of Syria and

Cilicia. Furthermore, Paul states, the churches of Judea did not even know him by sight, but only heard accounts of his dramatic transformation and glorified God because of what had taken place in Paul's life. In other words, neither is Paul under the influence of the Jerusalem church—or any of the Judean churches—nor is there any indication that anyone associated with these churches questions the legitimacy of his experience of God's grace. When they glorify God on account of him, they are affirming implicitly that their experience and understanding of the gospel is consistent with the "revelation of Jesus Christ" in Paul's life.

"Then I went into the regions of Syria and Cilicia, and I was still unknown by sight to the churches of Judea that are in Christ; they only heard it said, 'The one who formerly was persecuting us is now proclaiming the faith he once tried to destroy.' And they glorified God because of me."—Gal. 1:21–24

Paul's description of his second visit to Jerusalem (2:1–10), which took place fourteen years later, is much longer, perhaps because this meeting was both more contentious and more consequential. The general thrust of this account is consistent with what has preceded: the leaders of the Jerusalem church heard him describe the gospel he proclaims to the Gentiles, but "contributed nothing to him" (2:6), and recognizing the grace that had been given him, they offer Paul and his companions the "right hand of fellowship" ("koinonia," "partnership," "sharing"; 2:9). Moreover, this affirmation of Paul's gospel comes despite the troubling presence of "false believers," whom Paul depicts as secret agents intent on enslaving the Christians (2:4–5). Those with whom Paul consults do ask him to "remember the poor," i.e., to bear in mind the needs of the Jerusalem church itself, which Paul eagerly agrees to do. In other letters he mentions the collection he has been facilitating for "the poor among the saints at Jerusalem" (Rom. 15:26, cf. 1 Cor. 16:1–3, 2 Cor. 8:1–5), which Paul probably understood as a sign of the fundamental unity of the Jewish and Gentile elements of the church, as well as a way of honoring the church in Jerusalem (Georgi, *Remembering the Poor*). In short, there is no indication of any disagreement between Paul and the leaders of the Jerusalem church about the nature of the gospel or the authenticity of Paul's apostleship.

Within this account are a number of interesting details that help to clarify Paul's agenda in this portion of the letter. First, he suggests that his visit is "in response to a revelation" (2:2), i.e., not because he is being "called on the carpet" or for some reason needs to defend himself before the real authorities. Rather, it is God who initiates this meeting, which focuses on and affirms the essential unity of the developing Christ movement. Paul also says that when he describes (privately for the leaders) the gospel he proclaims to the Gentiles, he does so to make sure that he "is not running, or had not run, in vain." This, too, has to do with the question of the unity of the Church, for if the Jewish and Gentile branches of the church are unable to live in unity, then Paul's proclamation is effectively bankrupt. In other words, Paul's focus is on the unity of the church manifested in the acceptance by the leaders of the Jerusalem church of the Gentile mission.

Second, Paul mentions that he goes up to Jerusalem with Barnabas, another Jewish Christian evangelist among the Gentiles, and Titus, a Gentile convert. In the next section of the letter, Paul will tell of Barnabas' withdrawal from table fellowship with the Gentiles. For the moment, however, Barnabas is presented alongside Paul as a representative of the Antioch church, who, with Paul, helps prevent the theft of Christian freedom and is offered the right hand of fellowship (2:1, 5, 9). Titus is mentioned because of his status as a Gentile (a Greek, v. 3). Paul carefully notes that no one among the leaders at the meeting in Jerusalem finds it necessary for this Gentile to be circumcised, with the implication that there would also be no good reason for the Galatians to be circumcised. Neither the righteousness God seeks of us nor the quest for the unity of Christians requires circumcision. In fact, the imposition of practices such as circumcision represents a powerful threat to Christian unity, as Paul will later make clear (2:11–21, 5:2–12). The unity of the church is built on the gospel of grace, nothing else.

 Want to Know More?

About Titus? See Paul J. Achtemeier, ed., *HarperCollins Bible Dictionary,* rev. ed. (San Francisco: HarperCollins, 1996), p. 1158.

About Paul's time in Arabia? See Martin Hengel and Anna Maria Schwemer, *Paul between Damascus and Antioch: The Unknown Years* (Louisville, Ky.: Westminster John Knox Press, 1997).

Third, Paul describes his opponents at the meeting as "false believers secretly brought in," as "spies" on the "freedom we have in Christ Jesus," and as ones seeking to "enslave us" (2:4). Resisting them amounts to nothing less than a defense of the truth of the gospel (2:5). It is unclear who these "false brethren" were, what they were doing, and where they were. What is clear, however, is the association between freedom and the truth of the gospel. If these "spies," whoever they might be, are right, then freedom is a threat that must be contained and, moreover, the gospel is not true. How are Christian freedom and the truth of the gospel related? The true gospel that Paul preaches focuses on God's grace. God's grace liberates us not only from human patterns of domination and dependence, but also from the tyranny of sameness. Hierarchies exist precisely to impose order and conformity. Human quests to achieve unity by enforcing uniformity of thought and action—whether in morals, lifestyles, politics, or economics—go hand in hand with the denial of freedom. Paul understands that any proclamation of the gospel that denies the fundamental, singular sufficiency of God's grace will always result in the denial of freedom and lack of unity.

> **"False believers"**
>
> Gal. 2:4 refers to "false believers" or "false brothers" who were spying on Paul and Titus, "so that they might enslave us." Cousar says it is hard to determine from the Greek who these people were, but says Paul uses them to point out that the circumcision of a Gentile (in this case, Titus) under duress violates "the truth of the Gospel." (Cousar, 39–40) William Barclay notes that these "Judaizers," as they are sometimes called, believed that "before a man could become a Christian, he must be circumsized and take the whole law upon him." (Barclay, 16)

Fourth, the language Paul uses to describe those with whom he meets requires clarification. Twice he calls them "acknowledged leaders" (or "ones of repute" or, more literally, "ones who seem to be something"; 2:2, 6). Once he calls them "acknowledged pillars" (or, "those who are considered pillars"; 2:9). In 2:6 he speaks of "those who were supposed to be acknowledged leaders" (literally, "the ones seeming to be something"), and then adds an aside: "what they actually were makes no difference to me; God shows no partiality." It would be easy to misconstrue these references as disparaging the leaders of the Jerusalem church, as if Paul were trying to say that they weren't really worth much as leaders after all. But Paul is not seeking to denigrate the Jerusalem leaders. He clearly wants to affirm their authority as ones who agree with his sense of the gospel. The phrase "God shows no partiality" is the key to his real intent (Bassler). In the new creation that God has initiated in Jesus Christ, human distinctions melt away. When humankind falls down in worship before the crucified God, it does not matter what honors or status one has accumulated during a lifetime. Not even being a church leader or an apostle carries any weight

> "It is to be carefully noted that it is not a question of two different gospels being preached; it is a question of the same gospel being brought to two different spheres by different people specially qualified to do so." William Barclay, *The Letters to the Galatians and Ephesians*, rev. ed., Daily Study Bible (Philadelphia: The Westminster Press, 1976), p. 17.

with Paul, for any authority associated with such a position is derived from the power of the gospel itself, which continues to be the real focus of Paul's defense.

The claim that God is impartial is integrally related to Paul's later assertion that it is not our own righteousness or status—whether demonstrated by circumcision, piety and purity, leadership credentials, wealth, or worldly power—that secures our salvation, but the righteousness of Jesus Christ. The themes Paul has raised alongside his central argument for the independence and full integrity of the gospel he preached in Galatia serve a central concern—the unity of the church. First, Paul has affirmed God's initiative in everything that has happened, including the visits to Jerusalem. God's revealing grace, not human concerns, continues to be the driving force in all that he does. God's initiative and grace is the foundation for the real unity of the church (Cousar, 42f.). Second, Paul has made clear his independence from the Jerusalem leaders, while affirming their full agreement and partnership with him about the nature of the gospel. There is no hierarchy of power in the sphere of God's grace, only the good news that calls reconciled people together as one. Third, any denial of the truth of this gospel also constitutes a fundamental threat to human freedom in Christ. Both the unity of the church and the freedom of humans in Christ rest upon a singular point of agreement—the realization of God's grace. Christian freedom and unity must be worked for and preserved amidst the differences and conflicts of daily life, so that these become sites for the celebration of God's grace. Thus, Paul and the Jerusalem leaders did not decide to go their separate ways, but established and affirmed their unity through diverse ministries. They could not simply declare their oneness in theory and then look the other way when differences continued to arise. Forces both outside and inside the church continued (and continue) to threaten Christian freedom and unity, as the next section of this letter makes clear.

> "Two theological affirmations emerge [in this passage] worthy of further consideration. First, *the unity of the church is built on one gospel of grace. . . .*" Second, the *"one gospel of grace pushes Christians toward a visible unity."*—Charles B. Cousar, *Galatians*, Interpretation, 42.

? Questions for Reflection

1. Paul's faith is rooted in his experience of the "revelation of Jesus Christ" (Gal. 1:12). What is the significance for Paul and for the

Christian church that he had firsthand experience of Jesus? Paradoxically, as Paul focuses on freedom in Christ, church people have tried to impose his conversion experience as a model for others. Can you think of instances of this throughout history and in contemporary expressions of Christianity?

2. Paul is angry and frustrated. Not only has his message been challenged but his reputation has been attacked. Paul uses strong language when addressing the issue, yet addresses the Galatians as "brothers and sisters." Paul is passionate but does not make things personal. In what ways might Paul help us in dealing with our differences within our churches? Among Christian traditions? With those who reject Christianity?

3. Are there "versions of the Gospel" in our day that mistake cultural preferences for aspects of faithfulness (e.g., hair length, attire, nationalism)? How does one distinguish between the essence of the Gospel and cultural distortions? How "Christian" would a song like *God Bless America* or *America, the Beautiful* seem to Paul and other first-century Christians? To Christians in Third World countries? How is freedom in Christ, as Paul defines it, similar to and different from the kind of freedom we celebrate in our nation? That the world talks about?

4. Paul proclaims God's impartiality. Why is such a claim important to the situation of the Galatians? What has grace to do with God's impartiality? How might the belief in God's impartiality and grace affect how we relate within our congregations? Within our larger communities? How might the belief in God's impartiality and grace help us unite the Christian Church?

7

Table Fellowship at Antioch

We have seen in the preceding portion of Galatians that for Paul the unity of the church is based on nothing other than the good news of God's grace, a position with which the leaders of the Jerusalem church were in apparent agreement. As we listen to Paul's account of his meeting with the leaders of the Jerusalem church (2:1–10), one might imagine that harmony prevailed among these missionaries from that point forward. Paul now makes clear, however, that the oneness of Jews and Gentiles in the church was far from secure, and that even some of the leading figures in the Jerusalem meeting,

Cephas and Barnabas, were susceptible to divisive hypocrisy. It is easy to wonder after reading Paul's description of this conflict, however, whether he is not the one who incites the division. Paul's uncompromising tenacity as he presses Cephas concerning the implications of the gospel may put off many of us. Was there no room for compromise? The argument Paul mounts in this section of the letter (2:11–21) will help us see why he thinks the answer must always be a resounding "No!"

Peter and Paul

To make sense of this argument, we should note two aspects of how Paul argues here. First, Paul does not give any clear indication of where this section of the letter ends, at least not until the beginning of chapter 3, where he again clearly addresses the Galatians themselves. His report of what he said to Cephas (Peter) does not end in verse 14, as the punctuation in many modern English translations suggests, for Paul's statement at the beginning of verse 15 ("We ourselves are Jews by birth . . .") clearly indicates that he is still talking to Cephas, not to the (Gentile) Galatians. By the end of the chapter, however, it seems that he is no longer speaking to Peter but to the Galatians. Where, then, does the "transcript" of Paul's conversation with Peter end and Paul's additional theological reflections begin? Given the fact that even interpreters in the early church could not decide for certain, we can surmise that the people who first heard the letter in Galatia also couldn't tell for sure. Paul's skill in the art of verbal persuasion makes it likely that this "confusion" was intentional. In other words, Paul constructs his argument in this section so that it functions at two levels: as an account of what he said to Peter and, at the same time, as an argument delivered directly to the Galatian congregations. This two-level argument makes sense especially in light of the similarities between the two situations. In Galatia as in Antioch, the arrival of outsiders—advocates in both cases of a Judaizing form of Christianity—poses a challenge to the truth of the gospel Paul preaches and threatens the unity of the church. Paul knew that the agitators would probably still be present in Galatia as his letter was read. Thus, Paul makes the transition between his earlier words to Peter and his address to the outsiders in Galatia virtually imperceptible (Martyn, 230).

Gal. 2:11–13: Table Fellowship in the Church in Antioch

In Paul's time, Antioch—where the episode Paul relates is set—was among the three or four largest cities of the Roman Empire, a major trading center, and a city with mixed ethnic populations. Race riots aimed at the Jewish population occasionally erupted during this era. Because the church in Antioch was made up of both Jews and Gentiles, it was a setting in which the model of dual missions—one to Gentiles and one to Jews (cf. 2:9)—would be tested. How would peoples who had long histories of distrust, separation, and even violence now come together as one new people in the name of Christ? And how would they work out their differences around daily customs, such as food and table fellowship? Given the ethnic and cultural pluralism that is characteristic of life in many parts of North America today, along with our awareness of the conflicts that often arise as a result of such differences, it is not hard for most of us to imagine the pressures the Christian community in Antioch faced.

The conflict Paul describes focused on the question of whether Jewish Christians should continue to eat with Gentile Christians. The issue may have concerned what kind of foods were being eaten (i.e., Gentile foods probably would not have conformed to Jewish dietary strictures). But we also know from a wide range of Jewish and pagan sources that, while Jews and Gentiles did sometimes eat together informally, it was customary for most Jews to avoid sharing full meals with Gentiles (Esler, 93–116). Apparently, the meals taking place among the members of the Antioch church violated this norm. While it is not certain that these were eucharistic meals (i.e., "the Lord's Table"), which would probably have been full meals rather than the bread and juice of our modern custom (Lampe), the common meals in Antioch were at least eucharistic in spirit, in that they brought together Jews and Gentiles in a display of uncommon unity. We can presume from what Paul tells us that Jewish and Gentile Christians were eating together before Peter arrived and that he joined in these mixed meals for a period of time; the verb Paul uses to describe Peter's initial actions, "he used to eat with the Gentiles" (2:12), indicates repeated or customary actions.

Peter's partnership at table with the Gentile Christians ends when some people come from James, that is, from the Jerusalem church. Paul does not tell us what kind of pressure those who come from James put on Peter, only that he abruptly withdraws from shared table with Gentile Christians

---

Table Fellowship

In Antioch, Gentiles had for some time been welcomed into the church, even to the point of sharing common meals with Jewish Christians. (Some commentators suggest that these were meals at which the Lord's Supper was celebrated, but Cousar notes that there is nothing decisive in the text to support this view.) Up until this time there had been no divisive debate in Antioch about this "table fellowship," meals at which the categories of Jew and Gentile were clearly ignored.

Paul "saw certain things quite clearly. (i) A church ceases to be Christian if it contains class distinctions. In the presence of God a man is neither Jew nor Gentile, noble nor base, rich nor poor; he is a sinner for whom Christ died . . . (ii) Paul saw that strenuous action was necessary to counteract a drift which had occurred. He did not wait; he struck. It made no difference to him that this drift was connected with the name and conduct of Peter. It was wrong and that was all that mattered to him."—William Barclay, *The Letters to the Galatians and Ephesians,* rev. ed., Daily Study Bible, 19.

and that most or all of the rest of the Jewish Christians, including Barnabas, follow Peter's lead. According to Paul, Peter now kept himself separate from the Gentiles "for fear of the circumcision faction" (2:12). In other words, regardless of whatever other political forces, ethnic scruples, or theological convictions might have driven Peter and the others to withdraw, as far as Paul is concerned their actions are motivated primarily by fear. Twice in verse 13 Paul describes this behavior as hypocrisy ("play-acting") (Cousar, 48), which carries the sense of sharp discontinuity between word and action. Paul is not accusing Peter of being insincere, but of acting in a way that is not congruent with what he knows to be the truth. According to Cousar, Peter "is very sincere and is blind to the full impact of his actions" (Cousar, 49). As Paul puts it, "They were not acting consistently with the truth of the gospel" (v. 14). Paul confronts Peter "to his face" (2:11) and "before them all" (2:14).

> "It is important to recognize that the conflict with Peter, as far as Paul is concerned, is essentially a theological one. Paul gives no indications of a power struggle between warring factions in the early church . . . Neither is Paul's report of the incident intended to be a putdown of Peter . . ." Charles B. Cousar, *Galatians*, Interpretation, 48.

Why did Peter's withdrawal constitute a breach of the true gospel? Because it threatens the unity of the church in Antioch. By withdrawing from table with Gentile Christians, Peter essentially denies that he holds them to be full partners in God's grace. Regardless of the reasons that Peter found compelling, for Paul this action denies the truth of the gospel. It is clear here that Paul is not talking about doctrinal differences. He does not say that he and Peter disagree over what is the gospel; in fact, he has earlier established that they are in agreement about the gospel (2:7–9). His concern is not with "orthodoxy" ("right teaching"), but rather with what he calls "orthopody" (ortho = right or correct, and pod = feet; thus "walking rightly" or "acting consistently"). This verb is found nowhere else in the New Testament and only rarely in contemporary literature outside the New Testament. The truth of the gospel is threatened not only by wrong ideas, but by actions that deny it. Paul is not content merely to proclaim Christian unity but demands that it be practiced regardless of perceived threats. Anything short of this amounts to a denial of the gospel of God's grace.

> "The report of the incident serves to reiterate a point made in connection with 2:1–10: the gospel alone provides the bond for Christian unity. . . . Paul could never agree to unity if it necessitated compromising the gospel . . ."—Charles B. Cousar, *Galatians*, Interpretation, 49.

Gal. 2:14: Right Thinking and Right Walking

In 2:14 Paul begins to spell this out in more detail. His initial contention focuses on the question of ethnic identity. Even though Peter is a Jew, Paul points out, he has been living like a Gentile and not like a Jew. How, then, can he suddenly turn around and demand (implicitly) that Gentiles live like Jews? How, in other words, can he demand of Gentile Christians what he has not been practicing himself (i.e., Jewish dietary standards)? Paul's assumption here is that, in light of Peter's actions, in order once again to experience full fellowship with their Jewish sisters and brothers, the Gentile Christians would have to adopt the Jewish lifestyle again being practiced by Peter (Cousar, 47). Probably they would even need to be circumcised (cf. 2:12, where Paul refers to Peter's fear of the "circumcision faction"). For Paul this would mean that the unity of the church in Antioch would be based no longer on the grace of God but on the norms of Jewish ethnicity. The imposition of Jewish identity on Gentiles constitutes for Paul a denial of the sufficiency of God's grace.

Lest we think this is a concern peculiar to Paul's day, we need only remember that the church in our day continues to divide over a wide array of political and cultural issues. What might Paul say when we assume that "real Christians" organize themselves the way we do, or practice communion the way we do, or sing the same hymns, or salute the same flag, or vote for the same candidates we do? What would Paul say about the ethnic, racial, and class-based divisions that characterize the denominations of the modern church? We sometimes hear the claim that most of our divisions today are over matters of mere preference, rather than essentials, and thus that our divisiveness is more apparent than real. That way we can continue to associate with whomever we prefer and still regard ourselves as open-minded and ecumenical, fully in favor of (theoretical) unity. We need to remember, however, that Paul calls Peter (and the Galatians) to right walking (orthopody), not merely right teaching (orthodoxy). Theoretical unity does not measure up, nor does unity that is imposed from the top down or built upon sameness. The truth and power of the gospel is demonstrated in hard-won, self-sacrificial oneness, in unity that preserves the diversity of God's creation while standing up to the divisive forces of this world. The unity Paul seeks brings the gospel to fruition in everyday life, at common tables in Antioch, or Alexandria, or Atlanta.

In verse 15 Paul shifts his pronouns from "you" to "we," shifting his focus to what he and Peter share. His goal is to establish that the position taken by Peter in Antioch, and the position being promoted by the outsiders in Galatia, is untenable not only from Paul's vantage point but from the perspective of the Jewish Christian convictions they all hold in common. "We," he says, speaking to Peter (but in fact to all of his Jewish audience), "ourselves are Jews by birth and not Gentile sinners . . ." The reference to "Gentile sinners" is in part ironic, but also a typically Jewish way of referring to those who are neither circumcised nor keepers of the Law. The English translations break verses 15–16 into separate sentences, although in the Greek there is but one long sentence, focused on a threefold repetition of the contrast between being made right by the faithfulness of Jesus Christ versus "observance of the Law." In essence, Paul says, "Look Peter, because we (Jews who follow Christ) all know that 'a person is not made right (justified) by works of the law, but through the faith of Jesus Christ,' we have put our trust in Christ." Psalm 143:2 provides the Old Testament foundation for part of this assertion when it claims that no one is righteous before God (cf. Rom. 3:20). The affirmation that Christ is the true source of justification was held in common by all Christians, whether Jewish or Gentile.

> "We ourselves are Jews by birth and not Gentile sinners; yet we know that a person is justified not by the works of the law but through faith in Jesus Christ."—Gal. 2:15–16a

Then, in verses 17ff., Paul takes up a related concern that may have been raised by Peter, or by Paul's opponents in Galatia: What if, as a consequence of seeking to be justified (or made right with God and one another) in Christ, we break the Law and are found to be sinners? Is Christ then an agent of sinfulness? Two points help clarify the question and Paul's answer to it. First, when Paul speaks of "being made right" or "justified," he does not think only of the individual and his or her personal relationship with God, but of the whole of humankind with whom God is seeking to be reconciled (Cousar, 57–58). "Justification" thus entails the transformation of our relationships with one another, even the relationships between Jew and

> "Contemporary 'works of the law' may be defined as attitudes or activities which function in such a way as to usurp the grace of God; dispositions, whether religious or not, which aim to accomplish what the death of Christ accomplished. . . . In effect, salvation by works is an insidious form of idolatry. Its exponents refuse to acknowledge God as the true source of life, but instead turn themselves into gods, dispensers of salvation."—Charles B. Cousar, *Galatians*, Interpretation, 53.

Gentile, slave and free, male and female (3:28). In Antioch, table fellowship between Jewish and Gentile Christians was an embodiment of this unifying justification. Those who once were estranged now could experience relationships "made right." But precisely by embodying this "righteousness" or "justification" at table, the Jewish members of the church were transgressing the details of the Law and associating with "sinners." Was Christ, therefore, an agent of sin? "Absolutely not!" Paul answers. One can imagine contemporary circumstances that would raise similar concerns. Does the quest for unity lead Christians to relax their boundaries? In such cases, has Christ become an agent of sin? Ridiculous lines get drawn between Christians when faithfulness to Christ becomes adherence to rules.

Gal. 2:18–21: Christ and the Law

Paul continues his discussion of justification in verses 18–21. First (v. 18), he shifts the definition of transgression: building up again what had been already torn down, i.e., the walls separating people from one another, is what really makes us transgressors, for in doing so we deny God's grace. In the cases of Peter in Antioch and the agitators in Galatia, the reaffirmation of the Law's distinction between

> "I do not nullify the grace of God; for if justification comes through the law, then Christ died for nothing."—Gal. 2:21

Jew and Gentile would amount to a denial of the adequacy of Christ's death, for it would implicitly affirm that the route to reconciliation leads through keeping the Law. As Paul says at the end of this passage (2:21), this would mean that Christ died for nothing.

Then Paul turns to a complex series of assertions about the powers in whose realm he once lived and now lives: the Law and Christ. As he will later clarify, "through the Law" (or "on account of the Law") he has "died to the Law," so that he might live to God (or "for God" or "in God"), having been "crucified with Christ." It is difficult to know for certain what Paul means when he says that he has died to the law "through the Law," but he might have in mind the fact that Israel's leaders used the Law to condemn Jesus and put him to death. In any case, when Christ dies, the Law (or any other force in this life) no longer has any claim or power over him. So also, for Paul and every other Christian, being crucified with Christ means that no human institution—whether political principles or power, the Law, or even religion—has any ultimate claim on his life. In fact, Paul claims that he no longer has a life that is under his own will. He has effectively died. Now it is Christ who is the animating force in his life (2:20). The life he now conducts "in the flesh" (in contrast the realm of the "Spirit," upon which Paul will shortly focus attention; 3:1ff., 5:5, 5:16–26) is rooted in and shaped by his trust in the faithfulness of Jesus, the Son of God, whose power has been manifested in his sacrificial love and death for us. Verse 21 then summarizes Paul's whole argument since 2:15: Paul's teaching and practices affirm rather than nullify God's grace. Any attempt to reintroduce the divisive aspects of law-keeping into God's grace-filled means of setting the world right, in fact, nullifies grace by setting aside the effect of Christ's death.

We have already noted some of the ways this rich and provocative passage might speak to our contemporary conflicts in the church. Three additional points help both to clarify Paul's argument and make connections for us. First, Paul is addressing neither Judaism as a religion nor "legalists" (Cousar, 52), as has often been suggested. Nor does his argument imply that our actions ("works") have no place in God's work to make the world right again. Paul clearly is working very hard to preserve the integrity of the community in Galatia, and he understands that what we do in relationship with one another—even withdrawal from relationship—makes a difference. "It is just that when a work of the law, like circumcision, is urged on otherwise uncircumcised people to ensure their inclusion in the household of God, then what is the point of Christ's death?" (Cousar, 52). Christian history demonstrates that even our faith can become a source of division if it is regarded as a possession that secures membership or status within a restricted group.

This leads us, second, to be cautious as we consider passages such as Galatians 2:16, where most contemporary English translations render an ambiguous Greek phrase unambiguously as "faith in Jesus Christ" (twice in this verse). To preserve Paul's focus on the sufficiency of Christ's death for us, we would do well to remember that Paul is probably affirming that it is Christ's faithfulness ("the faith of Jesus Christ") through which God is setting the world right (Cousar, 53). This does not exclude the importance of our faith, however, but affirms that as we seek to conform our lives to the trusting faithfulness of Christ, we do so as an expression of God's grace rather than our own effort or merit. This is a crucial distinction. The discussion of Paul among the Protestant reformers often leads us to think that

Paul's main preoccupation during his ministry was the contrast between faith in Christ and works of law-keeping—i.e., differing patterns of human action. The key contrast for Paul, however, is what God has done versus what humans can do. Paul persistently stresses that the world has undergone a fundamental change because of what God has done in Christ. This is the central conviction that drives Paul's thinking.

Third, the faithfulness and justification of which Paul speaks is always social and corporate—not merely individual—in nature (Cousar, 57). Protestants often think of "justification" as God's answer to our personal sinfulness and guilt, of "righteousness" as a personal quality, and of "salvation" as a matter of our individual relationship with God. All of these distort and diminish what Paul and the early Christians would have understood by these terms. To be sure, God loves and redeems each of us as distinctive individuals, but God also loves the whole of creation and seeks not only reconciliation with isolated individuals but to "make right" the relationships between all people (Cousar, 56–58). The individualistic ways we have learned to think of God's redemptive work and our relationship with God are but one more symptom of the alienated and fragmented perceptions of broken humanity. Paul understands that our awareness of and participation in God's grace-filled actions to make the world right again demand that we be justified with others. God's grace does not leave us as isolated, albeit justified, individuals, but re-incorporates us in Christ as one new body. In this passage we have seen Paul argue strenuously about the religious and political implications of this corporate justification. In what follows, he will turn his attention to another dimension of this justified life: the experience of the Spirit.

 Want to Know More?

About the importance of Antioch to Christian theology? See Martin Hengel and Anna Maria Schwemer, *Paul between Damascus and Antioch: The Unknown Years* (Louisville, Ky.: Westminster John Knox Press, 1997), 279–286.

About Peter? See Paul J. Achtemeier, ed., *HarperCollins Bible Dictionary*, rev. ed. (San Francisco: HarperCollins, 1996), 833–836.

About the law? See Charles B. Cousar, *Galatians,* Interpretation (Atlanta: Westminster John Knox Press, 1982), 70–89.

? Questions for Reflection

1. How do you judge the position Paul takes with regard to Peter and the other Jewish Christians in Antioch? Why do you think Peter

might have thought it appropriate to withdraw from table fellowship with the Gentile Christians? Why did Paul see this action as a threat to the integrity of the gospel?

2. Paul and Peter are struggling to balance competing cultures and risks to their communities in light of the gospel. What risks might your congregation face should it take seriously the claim that Christ's grace is sufficient and his presence transcends culture? What kinds of issues have divided the church throughout its history, including the recent history of the North American church, your denomination, and your local congregation? To what extent do you think these issues have been similar to circumcision and dietary restrictions during Paul's time—that is, issues that are important within the religious framework of one group of Christians but that violate the gospel when imposed on others? Is division within the church inevitable? If so, what does that say about the sufficiency of Christ?

3. Which issues do you believe are important enough for you to break fellowship over? Why? Where do we draw the line between the quest for unity and respect for diversity and the quest for truth? Paul may have discovered that his policy of "being all things to all people" necessarily meant offending some people. When should people who have strong faith-based lifestyle convictions violate them for the sake of another? For example, should committed vegetarians eat meat to avoid offending hosts? How about those who vehemently oppose alcohol use? Should they share fellowship when alcohol is served? At interfaith gatherings, should Christians avoid the use of "Yahweh" because it is blasphemous to Jews to speak "the name that is above all names"?

4. The roots of Christianity are in a faith tradition that is communal. The New Testament writers know only of a "communal Christianity." To what extent do you think the individualism of our culture interferes with our full experience of the faith? How might we address this? Are there those in the world who might be able to be missionaries to us, teaching us what it means to be communal?

The Gospel, the Spirit, and Christian Identity

Contemporary media—especially TV, movies, and advertising—offer us a bewildering and bedeviling variety of images to copy as we seek to shape meaningful identities. We know who we are, supposedly, when we conform to one or another of the images set before us, even altering our self-understanding and self-expression from setting to setting, moment to moment, and mood to mood. While the issues surrounding identity in Paul's day may not have been quite so complex and confusing as they are today, many of the basic factors were quite similar. Then as now, most people learned to imitate others around them, especially by focusing attention on the rich and successful patrons of thriving households. Then as now, people assumed that humankind was divided into groups arrayed along a hierarchical spectrum, that it was important to mark the differences between the members of one's own group and others, and to conform to the expectations associated with each grouping. These patterns of differentiation marked the religious dimensions of life, just as they do today. In Galatians, Paul is fighting against such assumptions.

The Foundations of Christian Identity

As the third chapter begins, Paul turns from his own experience, which has marked much of the discussion in the first two chapters of the letter, to the Galatians' experience and to the foundational elements of their Christian identity. In 3:1–5:12 he will continue to develop the argument set forth in 2:15–21, introducing new themes alongside those announced earlier (Cousar, 64). The Spirit, freedom,

69

the promise of God, adoption as Abraham's children, and the purpose of the Law in God's plan all now receive focused attention. Throughout these chapters Paul is reaffirming the Galatians' identity, which rests in Christ alone. We need to be clear that Paul's argument is not against "legalism," or "Judaism," or the Jewish people, but against ways of shaping identity that are other than the revelation of Christ. To remind the Galatians of this faith they received, Paul appeals first to their own experience of the Spirit (3:1–5), then looks to the example of Abraham (3:6–14). He then moves on to discuss the role of the Law (3:15–29).

> "You foolish Galatians! Who has bewitched you? It was before your eyes that Jesus Christ was publicly exhibited as crucified! The only thing I want to learn from you is this: Did you receive the Spirit by doing the works of the law or by believing what you heard? Are you so foolish? Having started with the Spirit, are you now ending with the flesh?"—Gal. 3:1–3

Gal. 3:1–5: God's Transforming Gifts of the Spirit and of Faith

In this paragraph (3:1–5) Paul refers for the first time to the Spirit, which he will reintroduce from now on at decisive points in the argument (3:14, 4:6, 4:29, 5:5, 6:8). The Spirit will also feature prominently in Paul's discussion of freedom in 5:16–25. Paul's understanding of the Spirit is integrally related to his convictions that God has intervened in human history in Christ and brought into reality a new (apocalyptic) age (Cousar, 65ff.). The outpouring of God's Spirit was a key element in Jewish apocalyptic thinking, as was the transformation of relationships with God and with other humans. Paul has already made the important claim that his experience and understanding of the gospel of Jesus Christ came by "revelation" (i.e., by an "apocalypse"; cf. 1:12) and that his actions were at times guided by "revelation" (2:2). The apocalypse of Christ, in other words, has already altered Paul's own life in fundamental ways. Paul also recognizes that God's transformation of human life is taking place all around him, especially in the Spirit-endowed congregations he has helped found. Paul's question to the Galatians, "Who has bewitched you?" (3:1), presumes this apocalyptic framework.

Under the influence of the agitators in their midst and to Paul's amazement, the Galatians seem to be acting as if they had never heard or seen the dramatic story of Christ crucified (3:1). Did they receive the Spirit by works of the law or by the proclamation of Jesus Christ that leads to faith (3:2)? With this question, Paul seeks to return the Galatians to the beginning point in their life together as members of the Christian community. What more could they be striving for now? What could they hope to gain by means of practices he associates with "works of law"? Could they really be so foolish as to think that they could begin the walk of faith in the Spirit (the power of the new order) only to end it back under the powers of "the flesh"? That would mean that all of their experience of the Spirit was for nothing (3:4). Paul is mystified by their behavior: "Does God supply you with the Spirit and work miracles among you by your doing works of the law, or by the faith that comes from hearing the story of Christ proclaimed?" (v. 2, author's paraphrase).

> "Paul appeals to their beginnings as Christians, to their experience of entering the new age. How did they come to receive the Spirit, the supreme mark of the new age? By doing something, such as getting themselves circumcised, or by simply hearing the gospel which leads to faith?"—Charles B. Cousar, *Galatians*, Interpretation, 66.

Keeping with the emphasis throughout this letter on God's initiative in setting the world right, Paul affirms that it is God who supplies the Spirit to the Galatians, through faith rather than their actions (3:5). The presence of the Spirit cannot be secured through human means. Even the faith of which Paul speaks in these verses is a gift from God, not something over which we exercise choice. To be sure, we can decide to turn our backs on God, but we cannot will our own faith. Faith comes when God breaks into our world, whether by a revelatory vision, as in Paul's case, or by the revelatory power of Christ proclaimed. Twice in these verses Paul speaks of receiving the Spirit by "believing what you heard" (3:2, 5), a phrase that points to the faith elicited

> **Spirit**
>
> The Spirit, writes Cousar, is God's vital presence in the church and in the world. He lists four aspects of the Spirit that emerge from the questions Paul asks in these verses: 1) The Spirit comes in and with the preaching of the crucified Christ; 2) The Spirit is set in radical opposition to the flesh; 3) The Spirit is the power of the new age and thus the source of vitality and mighty works; 4) The Spirit comes to the whole community and not simply to a few select leaders. (See Charles B. Cousar, *Galatians*, Interpretation, 66–70.)

when the gospel is proclaimed (Martyn, 287ff.). In both instances Paul contrasts this trust-inducing, Spirit-endowing power of the gospel with the Galatians' attempts to observe the law. Perhaps Paul stresses this point in response to the agitators' efforts to convince the Galatians that obedience to the law is the real source of spiritual power. Paul wants the Galatians to know that nothing they have done or can do—whether circumcision, law-keeping, special liturgies, or even fervent prayer—assures the presence of the Spirit. The life-giving, transforming Spirit of God cannot be manipulated by human actions.

In this section Paul sets the Spirit in sharp contrast to "the flesh." Paul's opponents would likely have had little quibble with this point, but would have been shocked when he proceeded to associate "works of the law" with "the flesh" (Cousar, 67). This association might also surprise many Christians today, for we do not ordinarily associate religious practices with "the flesh." But, as Cousar puts it, " . . . the more sinister enemies of the faith are not always the obviously irreligious practices of the world but often the potent forces of morality and religion . . ." (Cousar, 67f.). What might Paul think about such pride-producing practices as tithing, going to church, feeding the poor, or public prayer? As in the case of circumcision or the observance of food laws, there is nothing pernicious about these acts in and of themselves—they may even make a positive contribution to the world. When they become markers of our identity, evidence of our "spirituality," or when they begin to function to set us apart from others in the church or our larger human family, they become "works of the flesh" and hindrances to grace. In short, not only obvious "irreligious practices," such as drunkenness, impurity, or licentiousness, but religious acts themselves may function as enemies of faith (Cousar, 67).

> "The terms 'spirit' and 'flesh' do not refer to parts of human nature but, rather, to two ways of living. The way of the flesh is self-centered rebellion and idolatry; it is not the way of the body or the individual as much as it is an orientation to the ways of the world. The way of the Spirit is life in bondage to the creator, in which Christ is freely acknowledged as Lord." —Art Ross and Martha Stevenson, *Romans*, Interpretation Bible Studies, 47–48.

Apocalyptic Thinking

A simple definition of apocalyptic thinking is that it is a way of thinking that affirms that God is guiding history to a final goal that God will bring about in the near future, in a particular way that has already been revealed. Revelation and Daniel are two examples of apocalyptic literature in the Bible. For a thorough discussion of apocalyptic language and thought, see M. Eugene Boring, *Revelation*, Interpretation (Louisville, Ky.: John Knox Press, 1989), 35–45.

How then do we discern the power of the Spirit? From Paul's writings in general it is clear that the Spirit of God is given to whole communities of faith for the sake of building them up in unity. Because God is one, God's Spirit is present to make such oneness a reality among humankind. Gifts are given to individuals not for their own personal edification, but to nurture the unity and witness of the church. In 1 Corinthians Paul makes this point with particular clarity while combating the tendency of members of that community to use their spiritual gifts to mark distinctions and establish hierarchies in their midst. Whenever some form of spiritual elitism begins to manifest itself in congregations, we can be sure that the Spirit of Christ is being denied in favor of self-justification—or "works of law," the designation Paul uses here in Galatians. We know that the Spirit of God is present when we observe the signs of liberation from bondage to the fallen order: love, joy, peace, patience . . . (Gal. 5:22)—always leading to the unity of the congregation.

Gal. 3:6–14: Abraham's True Descendents

Because Paul's teaching stands in tension with what the Galatians may have been hearing from his opponents, Paul justifies his claims in the verses that follow 3:1–5. He turns first (3:6–9) to an aspect of Christian identity that his opponents may have held forth in their teachings in Galatia, namely, the means by which Gentiles become children of Abraham. Jewish people, including both Paul and his opponents in Galatia, would have understood the inclusion of Gentiles among the people of God as the fulfillment of God's promise to Abraham (Genesis 12:3), which Paul cites in 3:8 (Cousar, 73–74).

But was Abraham's trust in God a matter of his own will and actions, i.e., something he brought with him to the relationship that compelled God to act in recognition of that faithfulness? Paul's goal in this paragraph is to deny this possibility as resolutely as he can, thereby overturning the agitators' claim that adoption into Abraham's family requires faithfulness to the covenant with Abraham as that is embodied in circumcision and the law.

Paul begins his case concerning descent from Abraham with a citation from Genesis 15:6 (Gal. 3:6), which in context affirms that God established Abraham's faith by means of the promise God first made to him that he would have a son. First came

> "Paul's logic in verses 6–14 goes like this: Since God reckoned his righteousness to Abraham by faith (so Gen. 15:6), then it is faith which distinguishes the true descendants of Abraham. His family is composed of persons who are set apart by belief, not by some other feature such as natural genealogy or the doing of the works of the law. . . . Abraham is not the father of circumcised Jews but of all persons, Jews and Gentiles, who accept God's grace in faith."—Charles B. Cousar, *Galatians*, Interpretation, 72–73.

the promise (God's act), which made it possible for Abraham to trust, and then the fulfillment of that promise in the birth of Isaac. Paul makes the same point even more clearly in Romans 4:20–22: Abraham did not "waver concerning the promise of God, but he grew strong in his faith as he gave glory to God, being fully convinced that God was able to do what he had promised. Therefore his faith was reckoned to him as righteousness." As a consequence, God's promise (to make a new people) is for those who, like Abraham, relate to God through faith (3:7). The precise expression Paul uses to designate these people—literally "the ones who are from faith"—stands in contrast to the phrase he used in 2:12 to designate those whose presence caused Peter to withdraw from table fellowship in Antioch ("the ones who are from circumcision" or "the circumcision"). In 3:10 he will use yet another, similar, phrase—"the ones who are from the law" ("who rely on the works of the law," NRSV)—to describe his opponents in Galatia. In each case, these phrases are shorthand designations of the fundamental, defining orientation and organizing focus of each group's identity. Were Paul to coin similar phrases for us today, he might speak of "the ones who trust in national power and might," or "the ones who rely on material goods for reassurance." In contrast to all idolatrous orientations, Paul affirms that Abraham and those who are his descendents shape their identities as "the ones who trust (God)." Those who receive the blessing of God are the people of faith who stand with faithful Abraham (3:9), not merely those who can trace their physical descent from Abraham. In these verses, then, we see Paul carefully redefining the basis of Christian identity, thereby overturning key aspects of his own identity prior to his experience of the revelation of Christ.

> "Even at his most involved, and here he is involved, one simple yet tremendous fact is never far from the mind and heart of Paul—the cost of the Christian gospel. He could never forget that the peace, the liberty, the right relationship with God that we possess, cost the life and death of Jesus Christ, for how could men ever have known what God was like unless Jesus Christ had died to tell them of his great love."—William Barclay, *The Letters to the Galatians and Ephesians,* Daily Study Bible, 26–27.

Faith and the Law

We should also note that as Paul speaks of Abraham's faith, he does not mention the sign that marked God's covenant with Abraham, circumcision, an omission his opponents would surely not have missed. Nor has he addressed the question of the law, which like circumcision was one of the identifying marks of the people of Israel, who regard themselves as Abraham's offspring and "heirs" of the promises God made to him. Paul turns to the question of the law with a complex argument that suggests both a negative role and a positive role for the law, which is commonly referred to as "the dual nature of the law." In 3:10–14, he argues on the basis of Old Testament texts that the law sets everyone under a curse—citing Deut. 27:26, for example: "Cursed is everyone who does not observe and obey all the things written in the book of the law." The agitators may have used this verse in their teaching in Galatia, in order to argue that even the Gentiles must strive to be obedient lest they remain under the curse. Paul, however, reinterprets the quotation, using it to argue that the law curses everyone, even those who try to live up to its requirements (Martyn, 324–28). In the end, everyone remains under the law's curse, Jew and Gentile alike. Paul does not say, as we may think, that the problem is that no one can really live up to all of the requirements. He says in Philippians 3:6 that he was blameless as to righteousness under the law, not implying thereby that he had never broken a commandment, however, but affirming that he had satisfied the law's demands (Cousar, 80). The key to Paul's reinterpretation of Deut. 27:26 lies rather in his citation alongside it of Habakkuk 2:4 ("The one who is righteous will live by faith"). Habakkuk 2:4 is the only other passage in the Old Testament besides Genesis 15:6 (with which Paul began this portion of the argument in 3:6) that refers to both faith and righteousness (Martyn, 312). On the basis of this verse, Paul can affirm that no one is made right by means of the law, which can only set humankind under a curse. "The law from the beginning has indicated only one way of salvation, and that is something done by God and not by humans. The person who *really* keeps the law realizes that the law can never justify and so puts his trust in the faithfulness of God" (Cousar, 74–75).

> "The law is instructive for the Christian community as it lives out its life in the world. Christians are no longer 'under the law' (5:18) but nevertheless can be guided by the law in facing all sorts of moral and ethical dilemmas."—Charles B. Cousar, *Galatians*, Interpretation, 82.

Paul's next statement makes a point to which he will return in 3:19–20, namely, the law does not have its origins in faith (3:12). Probably anticipating his opponents' use of Leviticus 18:5 to contradict the argument he has just made, Paul cites a version of this text here ("whoever does the works of the law will live in them"), but in order to refute it (Martyn, 328–34). Paul has just said, citing Habakkuk, that faith is the means through which life is made right. Leviticus 18:5, in contrast, claims that life comes through obedience to the law. In the churches Paul has founded, including the churches of Galatia, Paul the Jew has seen abundant evidence that faith, not the commandments, makes the world right. But to refute the contrary claim of Leviticus, Paul returns to the root of the faith he shares with his opponents and the Galatians—that is, to Christ himself. What is it that sets humankind free from the curse of the law under which we all live? What is it that makes "life made right" possible? Paul, the Galatians, and the agitators in Galatia all know as Christians that Christ's death on the cross is the answer to both questions.

In verse 13 Paul cites yet another Old Testament text, Deut. 21:23, in order to affirm that when Christ died on the cross, he stood under a curse, just as all of humankind stands under the curse of the law. As Paul says, Christ became a curse for us, both Jew and Gentile. That is, he took our place under the curse, precisely in order to rob the law of its continuing power to hold humanity—whether Jew or Gentile—under its power. In this way, Christ made it possible for the blessing of Abraham, "the promise of the Spirit through faith" (3:14), to come to the Gentiles. Here Paul returns to the place he began the argument back in 3:1–5: the Galatians' experience of the Spirit. The Spirit comes not through our own accomplishments, our own attempts to make the world right, but through the realization in Christ of the promise made to Abraham, a promise realized only when the powerful curse of the law has been broken. There is no room for a return to life under the demands of the cursing law.

Want to Know More?

About Jewish apocalyptic thinking? See Calvin J. Roetzel, *The Letters of Paul: Conversations in Context* (Louisville, Ky.: Westminster John Knox Press, 1998), p. 196 n. 68; *Interpreter's Dictionary of the Bible* (Nashville: Abingdon Press, 1962), 1:157–61.

About the Spirit? See Charles B. Cousar, *Galatians*, Interpretation (Atlanta: John Knox Press, 1982), 66–70.

About spirit and flesh? See Art Ross and Martha Stevenson, *Romans*, Interpretation Bible Studies (Louisville, Ky.: Geneva Press, 1999), 47–49; Paul J. Achtemeier, *Romans*, Interpretation (Atlanta: John Knox Press, 1985), 131–37.

As we noted earlier, this is a complex and difficult section of the letter, but one in which essential elements of Paul's thinking come to light. He has now made clear that the law itself both 1) points to Christ's faithfulness as the fulfillment of God's promise to Abraham and 2) stands against faith, both as an alternative pattern for life and as a cursing power that holds humankind captive. In the paragraphs that follow in chapters 3 and 4, Paul will continue to press his case.

By placing all of humankind—whether Jew or Gentile—under the curse of the law, Paul also prepares the way for his claim that all now stand together—redeemed from the law's curse—on the same footing, which is faith in Christ. Nothing else is needed. Whatever might be added to this foundation calls into question the sufficiency of Christ, and will, moreover, threaten the unity of church.

? Questions for Reflection

1. What are the most important and most common means by which we shape and express our identities today? How does our culture expect to shape our identities? How does Paul's perspective on the foundations of Christian identity differ from the alternatives offered by the media?
2. Why does Paul think the Galatians have been "bewitched"? What forces or ideals bewitch us today? Why does Paul emphasize the Galatians' foundational experience of the Spirit? What are your foundational faith experiences? What are the foundational experiences of your church? Do they still define who you are?
3. Is faith a gift from God or our response to the gospel (or both)? What difference might it make to claim that faith is a gift rather than something we control?
4. In what sense might our religious practices in fact be "works of the law," as Paul understands things? What religious practices do we put the most emphasis on? How do your religious practices distinguish you from others in your thinking? In God's eyes?

9 Galatians 3:25–4:11

New Life in Christ versus Enslavement to the Powers

Ten times in Galatians 3 through 5 Paul describes the human condition as being "under the power of" enslaving forces, including "a curse," "sin," "the law," "disciplinarians, guardians, and trustees," and "the elements of the cosmos" (3:10, 22, 23, 24–25; 4:2, 3, 4, 5, 21; 5:18). Paul apparently wants to remind the Galatians that without the faith of Christ all humans live as slaves to idolatrous powers (Martyn, 370–73). Because Paul categorizes both sin and the law as enslaving powers, it is clear that one's religious orientation and rituals make no difference. In other words, human religion, even Israel's religion, has no power to set us free. Paul's argument here poses a sharp challenge to a culture such as our own, where we proclaim and celebrate both religious freedom and the freedom of the individual.

Gal. 3:25–29: Baptism and New Identity

In 3:23–25 Paul brings his discussion of the law to a temporary close, arguing that the law was a "*custodian*" (or "disciplinarian" NRSV)—a household servant charged with conducting children to and from school—that kept humankind "imprisoned and guarded," preparing for Christ's coming (3:23–24). In these verses he depicts humankind as children subject to external authorities, an image he will further develop in the first seven verses of chapter 4. But in verse 26 he shifts from the perspective of children under an imprisoning, hostile power to the claim that "in Christ Jesus you are all children of God through faith."

Paul focuses the Galatians' attention once again on their own experience. This time he reminds them of the language and imagery of their baptisms, probably drawing on the liturgical traditions used in Paul's churches: "As many of you as were baptized into Christ have clothed your-selves with Christ." Paul cites this rich, provocative tradition here because he is still working to remind the Galatians of their identity in Christ, and no other practice so clearly affirms the distinctive

> "There is no longer Jew or Greek, there is no longer slave or free, there is no longer male and female; for all of you are one in Christ Jesus."—Gal. 3:28

and radically new identity of the followers of Christ. When he speaks of the baptized clothing themselves in Christ (3:27), he recalls the way they were stripped of their old clothing prior to baptism and clothed anew as they emerged from the water, symbolizing putting aside the old person who was held in bondage to evil powers (cf. Col. 3:9). As they put on the new clothing, they "put on Christ," being transformed and conformed to his image, and joined the community as "members" of his body. Paul intends this imagery to remind the Galatians that their complete incorporation into this new power and realm of existence was evidenced at their baptisms, requiring nothing further to complete their identification with Christ in faith.

Paul is also interested, however, in the portion of the baptismal tradition that accompanies the act of baptism itself: "There is no longer Jew or Greek, there is no longer slave or free, there is no longer male and female; for all of you are one in Christ Jesus." The named pairs represent the primary distinctions by which humankind in Paul's day was described and relationships were ordered. When (per-haps at baptism) these pairs are said no longer to exist, the depend-able (and enslaving!) order of the world effectively ceases to have power over those who are baptized (and thus the gathered congrega-tion, as well). Baptism means, then, that the religious and ethnic dis-tinctions between Jew and Gentile, the very distinctions that had shaped so profoundly Paul's own life prior to his experience of the revelation of Jesus (1:11–24), no longer have any meaningful refer-ence. As Paul will affirm in the conclusion of this letter, "neither cir-cumcision nor uncircumcision is anything; but a new creation is everything!" (6:15, cf. 2 Cor. 5:17). Thus, by reminding the Gala-tians of their baptisms, Paul continues to reconfirm the bases of Christian identity, demonstrating that, through God's faithful ful-fillment of the promises in Christ, Jews and Gentiles now belong together without distinction as one people, "for all of you are one in Christ Jesus" (3:28).

Gal. 4:1–8: Not Only Children, but Heirs

At the beginning of chapter 4, Paul returns to his analogy between humankind and children, focusing now on the case of "the heir" (Cousar, 90). This example presumes knowledge of the family structure of ancient Mediterranean culture, where children indeed were typically regarded as household property, with rights equivalent to those of a slave. So when Paul says that heirs, so long as they are minors, are no better than slaves, and that they remain under the power of guardians and trustees until a time determined by the father (4:1–2), he refers to widespread social, economic, and legal customs of the Roman Empire. The heir does have the prospect, however, of one day inheriting the whole household (4:1). Paul compares human life ("we" includes both Jews and Gentiles) prior to the revelation of faithful Christ to being a minor, held in bondage under "the elemental spirits of the world" (4:3). But this was true only until "the fullness of time had come," when God sent his Son into the world (4:4).

> **"You are all children"**
>
> In the New Testament world, children typically slept with nursemaids or custodians, rather than in the same quarters as their parents. Under Roman law, male children, even the eldest son, remained under the authority of their fathers, regardless of age or marital status, until the father died. Fathers held the legal right even to take their children's lives.

Paul emphasizes Jesus' full humanity (born of a woman) and full identification with the human condition (born under the law) in order to affirm that Jesus overcomes the enslaving powers not from outside the system but from within. Like the rest of humankind, he is held captive under the elemental spirits of the world (under the law as a Jew) (Cousar, 94–95). God sends Jesus Christ into the world for no other reason than to accomplish the liberation of humanity from the enslaving powers.

> "And because you are children, God has sent the Spirit of his Son into our hearts, crying, 'Abba! Father!' So you are no longer a slave but a child, and if a child then also an heir, through God."—Gal. 4:6–7

At the end of verse 5 Paul leaves for a moment the image of the heir and picks up the language of adoption. Again, by using "we" Paul affirms the common status of Gentiles (i.e., the Galatians) and Jews. Both groups become members of God's family through the faith of Jesus Christ (Cousar, 92). When in 4:6 Paul writes of the Spirit, saying, "God has sent the Spirit of his Son into our hearts, crying, 'Abba! Father!' " he uses both the Aramaic (the language spoken in Paul's day by Jews in Palestine) and Greek words for "Father," reinforcing the oneness of Jews and Gentiles.

Paul summarizes in verse 7: "So you are no longer a slave (*i.e., held captive under the powers*) but a child (*a full member of God's family*), and if a child then also an heir (*i.e., a recipient of the promised Spirit*), through God." Therefore, no reason exists for the Galatians to add anything to their Christian identities, for it has been accomplished "through God."

> "Christ's death as a means of salvation excludes all other means; he creates one community, not many; thus there can no longer be barriers separating otherwise disparate groups. Circumcision implied division between Jew and non-Jew and between male and female. Baptism into Christ means unity."—Charles B. Cousar, *Galatians*, Interpretation, 85.

Gal. 4:8–11: "How Can You Turn Back . . . ?"

In the next paragraph (4:8–11) clues are provided as to other aspects of law the Galatians have been observing. Paul's astonishment is revealed again in the question: how could they turn back again to "weak and beggarly elemental spirits" (cf. 4:3), in this case, specifically, the law and what it represents?

Paul describes the shift he sees now taking place under the influence of the agitators as a "conversion" ("turn back again," v. 9) to the old way of living. Paul is concerned about the Galatians' adoption of special (sacred) days, months, seasons, and years. The observance of these special times represents one aspect of the human tendency to divide experience into holy and unholy, sacred and secular times and places. Two primary problems are associated with this impulse. First, Paul apparently understands these practices as expressions of human religion, that is, as an attempt to know God (or the gods) on our terms and even to manipulate the relationship to our benefit. But Paul has just noted that one of the distinctive elements in the Galatians' experience of God was that they had come not only to know who God is, but, more important, to be known by

 Want to Know More?

About who the agitators were? See Charles B. Cousar, *Galatians*, Interpretation, 5–6.

About family relations in New Testament times? See Carolyn Osiek and David L. Balch, *Families in the New Testament World: Households and House Churches* (Louisville, Ky.: Westminster John Knox Press, 1997), 42–43.

> "I am afraid that my work for you may have been wasted."—Gal. 4:11

God. They have been adopted and now inherit the promised Spirit not because they know God through a religious quest, but because God knows them (by sending the Son into the world, born of a woman, born under the law; 4:4). Whatever they know about God, moreover, is the result of God's revelation to them in Jesus Christ, not their religious pursuit of the sacred through practices that divide creation into sacred and profane.

There are four motifs of theological significance in 4:1–11, says Cousar: 1) God is the prime figure, who determines the right time for the new age to break into the old; 2) Jesus was fully human, with all the consequences that came with that; 3) God sent the Spirit of God's son to confirm the new status of being God's children; 4) Paul's writing in verses 4–6 raise the question of whether he is reflecting on the relationship of Father, Son, and Holy Spirit. (See Charles B. Cousar, *Galatians*, Interpretation, 93–98.)

Second, the very division of the world into sacred and profane times and places effectively limits the reach of God's power. One of the remarkable aspects of early Christian practices was the refusal to identify sacred places or times. Rather than meeting in the Temple or other "sanctuaries," they met in mundane households. They confessed that God was present not in predetermined times or places, but wherever and whenever two or three gathered in the name of Christ (cf. Matthew 18:20). As Paul himself says to the Corinthians, their body, by which he means the gathered community (not just their individual, physical bodies), is the temple of the Holy Spirit (1 Cor. 3:16–17, 6:19; 2 Cor. 6:16). In short, Paul regards the trappings of human religion, including the practices being adopted by the Galatians under the influence of Paul's opponents, as symptoms of a tragic return (a "re-conversion") to enslavement under the elemental powers of the broken creation. For this reason, he ends the section on a pessimistic note, wondering whether his effort among the Galatians has been wasted (4:11).

"Jesus Christ did not say, 'I am come that they may have religion,' but 'I am come that they may have life, and have it abundantly.' To make religion a thing of special times is to make it an external thing. For the real Christian every day is God's day. It was Paul's fear that men who had once known the splendour of grace would slip back to legalism, and that men who had once lived in the presence of God would shut him up to special days."—William Barclay, *The Letters to the Galatians and Ephesians*, Daily Study Bible, 37.

In a culture in which we have learned to regard sin as a matter of individual choices and actions, as things we choose to do or not to do, we may find strange and challenging Paul's talk of "elemental powers" that control us. Yet, while Paul's perspectives may not conform to the language we have learned to speak in the churches of North America, we may nonetheless decide that he has something to teach us, especially as we pause to consider our own experience. Have we, for example, found satisfaction in our own religious quests—whether pursued in the name of Christianity, spirituality, piety, or social justice—to secure our salvation before God? Have our own ways of defining individual and religious identities wrought freedom and unity among the people of God, or do we remain captive to the same powers, and touched by the same alienation and hostility, that we see so prominently in the culture around us? The faith to which Paul directs his readers' attention offers not just another religious alternative, but a fundamentally different diagnosis of and prescription for the human condition, one that offers both the possibility of real freedom and a wholly new way of being human together.

 ## Questions for Reflection

1. What does Paul mean when he says that in Christ "there is no longer Jew or Greek, there is no longer slave or free, there is no longer male and female" (3:28)? What did these terms designate in Paul's day? What contemporary parallels might we identify? In what sense does the revelation of Jesus Christ break down such distinctions?

2. How are we held captive to the powers of this world? What has religion to do with such powers? What or who are the powers of this world (or "the elemental spirits")? Why would the Galatians have been tempted to turn back toward the powers of their day? How might we also be so tempted?

3. In Gal. 4:10 Paul challenges the Galatians' observation of "special days, and months, and seasons, and years." What do you think he has in mind by these terms, and what about these practices threatens the Christian faith of the Galatians? In what ways do we today divide our experience of the world into sacred and profane, holy and unholy? Would Paul challenge our assumptions and practices in these matters? What difference do such divisions make with regard to our sense of mission? What difference do such divisions make with regard to our understanding of the function of church buildings or shopping malls, for example?

The Vocation of Freedom in the Daily Life of Congregations

Throughout Galatians we have observed a variety of arguments Paul uses to refocus the Galatian congregations' identities around the gospel they received. Paul's own call-ing, the Galatians' experi-ences, the law, analogies from daily life, and scrip-ture all figure promi-nently in the case the apostle sets before the Galatians. Running like a thread through all of these aspects of Paul's argument is his convic-tion that in Jesus Christ God has commenced a "new creation" (6:15), with the consequence that God's Spirit is now in the world in a new way, transforming those whose lives are shaped by the faith of Jesus. The gospel that Paul first preached to the Galatians was a gospel of deliverance (1:4), but others brought a message of the need for Gentiles to fulfill the Law. The Galatians failed to see the threats entailed in this message, and adopted some of their practices. Thus, as Paul draws this letter to a close, he focuses on the issue of freedom, the gift of God most clearly under threat in the churches of the Galatians.

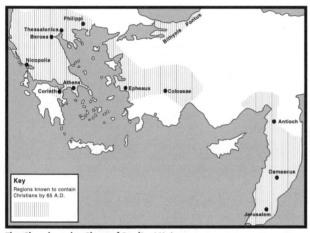

The Church at the Close of Paul's Ministry

Making Sense of Paul's Ethics Today

The last major portion of the body of this letter (5:13–6:10) is often described as the ethical component in Paul's argument, as here he unpacks the implications of the theological teaching he has provided in the rest of the letter. We should be careful, however, not to drive too sharp a wedge between the theological and ethical portions of Paul's letters (Cousar, 122), because, for Paul as for most New Testament writers, beliefs and practices are inseparable, since faith incorporates the whole of life—attitudes, words, priorities, values, and actions. When we, in contrast, separate our practices from our beliefs, we run the risk of reducing faith to proposals we adhere to intellectually or things we merely talk about in church.

We also risk distorting Paul's pastoral instructions if we treat them as rules universally applicable to all times and places. Taking Paul seriously requires that we be sensitive to the particular cultural and historical contexts in which he wrote, and especially to the particular problems he addressed. Paul wrote to real people in real situations, as this letter has made abundantly clear. He does not have in mind, nor could he have imagined, many of the problems faced by Christians and congregations today. On the other hand, it is also important not to dismiss Paul's ethical teachings as outdated or inapplicable to our situations. Paul addresses fundamental human issues that take different shape in different times and settings. We must learn to read Paul's teachings fully within the context to which they were addressed, and then appropriate his teachings in terms of the issues and concerns facing us now.

> "Paul does not offer a set of moral principles, universally valid, which only need to be adjusted slightly and then applied to the modern context. . . . Due to the social, cultural, and political gaps between the ancient and modern worlds, it is rarely possible to find in the biblical text instant solutions to the moral dilemmas of the twentieth century."—Charles B. Cousar, *Galatians*, Interpretation, 124–125.

As we begin to look at this section of the letter to the Galatians, it may look like Paul is practicing what he has preached against earlier in the letter. He offers relatively detailed instructions for daily life, but the directions he gives the Galatians do not constitute "another law." Instead they are descriptive, concrete examples of the daily life of faith.

The key concepts in this section of the letter are "freedom," "love," and "mutual responsibility," i.e., bearing one another's burdens (6:2). These terms are integrally related: love is the true expression of freedom (Cousar, 123), and bearing one another's burdens is the concrete expression of freedom and love. In effect, in this section Paul asks his readers to take a look at themselves and those around them, to observe the kinds of behavior that dominate their life together, and discern which power—the "flesh" or the "Spirit of God"—is at work among them.

On Freedom

As Paul claims in chapter 6 (in a maxim well-known in our culture), we "reap what we sow" (6:7–10). The produce harvested manifests the nature of the seed planted. The Galatians are apparently now harvesting discord, enmity, competition, and chaos—the produce that has grown from the seeds planted by the agitators. While we do not learn from Paul the precise nature of the problems that have beset the congregations of Galatia, it is clear that Paul regards these "presenting issues" as symptoms of a shift away from the gospel. He understands that there is an integral connection between the faith (or lack thereof) the Galatians embody and the freedom, peace, and joy (or lack thereof) they experience in their daily lives. His interest in refocusing the Galatians' identity on the faithfulness of Christ now finds concrete expression in his observations about the practices that make up the daily life of their community.

> "Freedom is not a commodity obtained and stored away for a rainy day; it is a gift which increases its value in the using and can be lost through misuse."—Charles B. Cousar, *Galatians,* Interpretation, 122.

The first paragraph in this section, 5:13–15, begins with a reaffirmation of the assertion Paul made in 5:1:

"For freedom, Christ has set us free.   "For you were called to freedom . . ."

(5:1)   (5:13)

While Paul follows the assertion in 5:1 with a warning not to submit again to the yoke of slavery (i.e., circumcision), in 5:13 he focuses on the dangers of misusing freedom as an "opportunity for self-indulgence." The word translated by the editors of the NRSV as "opportunity" could refer to a "base suitable for military operations" (Cousar, 129; Martyn, 485; Longenecker, 70–74). In addition to the issues related to adherence to the Law, the Galatians are also facing dissension regarding the issue of freedom in Christ. Apparently there are those among the Galatians who have interpreted "freedom" as the opportunity to act without restraint. As Paul suggests, the Law, while intended by God for the good of humankind, can be used in ways opposed to God's will, so too he suggests can freedom be put to use for purposes opposed to God's will—that is, as a *base camp* for "self-indulgence."

Continuing with the military analogy, we could say that the alternative to this corruption of the gift of freedom is to embark on campaigns of mutual servanthood, employing love as the vehicle ("but through love become slaves to one another" 5:13) (Longenecker, 185). Such love and servanthood, Paul says, is actually that which confirms and provides the correct interpretation of the Law! (See Cousar, 131f). This love is not merely a generalized attitude of benevolence toward others, but real actions of care, compassion, and solidarity toward real people, actions that address women and men in their particularity and in the specific concreteness of their life situations (Cousar, 132).

In the Sermon on the Mount, Jesus taught us that loving others who already love us is no great accomplishment. He calls on his disciples to love even their enemies, in this way becoming mature and complete ("perfect" or "finished"), just as God is (Matthew 5:43–48). The love Paul describes in this letter demands no less of us, for living in and being guided by the Spirit (5:25) will manifest itself in our dealings even with competitors (5:26) and transgressors (6:1). Although Paul's immediate concern is with the relationships among the Galatians, the ethic he espouses has far-reaching implications (Cousar, 132). God's love reaches into the world wherever there is alienation, exploitation, oppression, or abuse, and makes the world right again.

Whereas people in North American culture often treat freedom as a matter of individual rights, and love as a personal experience associated with emotional and sexual expression, Paul understands freedom and love as signs of the Spirit's presence, discovered and practiced in human community. As long as division and strife, partisan spirits, competition, or claims of superiority (5:15, 26) dominate the life of a community, there is no real freedom, and certainly no love. In contrast, Paul teaches that the preservation of freedom depends on realizing and nurturing God's gifts of patience, generosity, gentleness, self-control, and the other fruits of the Spirit (5:22–23) (Cousar, 125).

> "Now the works of the flesh are obvious: fornication, impurity, licentiousness, idolatry, sorcery, enmities, strife, jealousy, anger, quarrels, dissensions, factions, envy, drunkenness, carousing, and things like these. I am warning you, as I warned you before: those who do such things will not inherit the kingdom of God."—Gal. 5:19–21

Gal. 5:19–26: Works of the Flesh and Fruit of the Spirit

Perhaps the most familiar verses in this section are the "works of the flesh" and "fruit (singular) of the Spirit" described in 5:19–26, which sound like ancient lists of "vices and virtues." Paul presents these not as individual qualities the Galatians are to cultivate, but as marks or signs that distinguish daily life in the power of the Spirit. Paul is describing the kind of life that God now offers in the Spirit. The "works of the flesh" Paul lists (5:19–21) are not merely individual vices, but practices that tear at the fabric of the community. Over half of these fifteen items relate explicitly to social conflicts (e.g., enmities, strife, dissensions, etc.). Even the sexually oriented symptoms Paul lists in 5:19—fornication (sexual unfaithfulness), impurity (violent sexual activity), and licentiousness (prideful displays of debauchery) (Martyn, 496)—are, in fact, socially disruptive.

> "By contrast, the fruit of the Spirit is love, joy, peace, patience, kindness, generosity, faithfulness, gentleness, and self-control. There is no law against such things. And those who belong to Christ Jesus have crucified the flesh with its passions and desires. If we live by the Spirit, let us also be guided by the Spirit."—Gal. 5:22–25

The flesh and the Spirit are at war. But while the works of the flesh produce social violence, the fruit the Spirit produces does not combat this violence with still more powerful violence. God's refusal to meet violence with violence stands in contrast to human wars, as well as to foundational myths depicted in the cartoons, TV programs, and movies our culture thirsts for (Wink, 17–25). The fruit of the Spirit is a cornucopia of practices and attitudes that build up the community and manifest God's oneness and self-giving love. Only amidst this kind of produce, only within the reign of God (5:21), is freedom possible. And only the freedom God offers when we become servants of one another in the faith of Christ produces this kind of oneness—relationships made right—in human community.

> "What Paul means by the flesh needs a certain bit of translation for contemporary Christians. He is not saying that material things are inherently evil, nor is he implying that human feelings, physical desires, or sensual pleasures are themselves to be avoided or suppressed. What makes the flesh so destructive is that it can become the norm by which people's lives are lived."—Charles B. Cousar, *Galatians*, Interpretation, 137.

Slavery and Freedom in the Shadow of the Cross

At first glance we may regard Paul's association of freedom and slavery for the sake of our neighbor (5:13) as an impossible contradiction, especially since, following the parallel assertion of freedom in 5:1, he has warned the Galatians not to submit again to the yoke of slavery. In the earlier context, of course, his warning is focused on the slavery imposed by circumcision and the Law. In 5:13–15, however,

Paul has in mind the kind of slavery that comes through submission of one's will and actions to God. Paul understands that human life—part of the created order—is never free of subjection to power. Freedom is not a matter of autonomy and absolute independence, as many in our culture think of it, but a question of whether one submits—consciously or not—to the fallen, enslaving, death-dealing powers of the world ("the flesh") or to a merciful, loving God who has brought the Law to completion in the cross of Christ.

> "Scholars have long recognized . . . that the lists of virtues and vices such as the ones in Gal. 5:19–23 were quite popular in the Hellenistic world. . . . While such lists may have come to Paul either through Hellenistic Judaism or through the Hellenistic church, they go back to Greek philosophy. Except for 'love,' the virtue list contains nothing that would be unusual in a catalog of conventional Greek ethics. The way these virtues are subordinated to the Spirit and thus given an eschatological dimension, however, is Paul's own doing."—Calvin Roetzel, *The Letters of Paul: Conversations in Context,* 14.

As always for Paul, the cross is never far from sight; here it is the model that stands at the heart of all of Paul's directives in this section of the letter (cf. 5:11, 5:24, 6:12, 6:14). As Paul says in his summation of the contrast between "works of flesh" and "fruit of the Spirit," "those who belong to Christ Jesus have crucified the flesh with its passions and desires" (5:24). In other words, in our identification with Christ on the cross, we participate in his conquest of the powers that seek to hold us captive. Set free from these powers and granted the gift of life in the Spirit (5:25), we take up new identities as servants of the crucified Christ. Human freedom, thus, is bound inextricably to identification in servanthood with the one who, through his death for us on the cross, has overwhelmed the enslaving powers, whether sin (3:22), law (3:23ff.), the elemental spirits of the world (4:1–11), or death itself. Becoming slaves to one

 Want to Know More?

About spirit and flesh? See Art Ross and Martha Stevenson, *Romans,* Interpretation Bible Studies (Louisville, Ky.: Geneva Press, 1999), 47–49; Paul J. Achtemeier, *Romans,* Interpretation (Atlanta: John Knox Press, 1985), 131–37.

another through love (5:13–14), restoring one another in gentleness (6:1), and bearing one another's burdens (6:2) are both the symptomatic practices of servants of Christ and the marks of true human freedom.

? Questions for Reflection

1. What is the proper relationship between what we believe and what we do as Christians? How closely are our ethical stances related to

our theological convictions? How closely do our actions reveal what we claim to believe?

2. What kinds of actions or behavior does Paul understand as the "fruit of the Spirit"? What distinguishes the "fruit of the Spirit" from "works of the flesh"? How does Paul's use of the term "flesh" differ from how the word "flesh" is used in our culture? Can you suggest a better English translation?

3. Is the fruit of the Spirit something we impose on ourselves as virtues? Does the fruit of the Spirit manifest itself in primarily individual or communal ways? Is the battlefield imagery a helpful one today? What other images might describe the relationship between the fruit of the Spirit and the works of the flesh?

4. Paul argues that the Law was an instrument intended by God for good but co-opted by the forces opposed to God and thus destructive of human community. So also he argues that even Christian freedom can be co-opted for purposes opposed to God's will. What other aspects of the Christian faith have been co-opted and used for purposes opposed to God's will? Paul calls the Galatians (and us) to "bear one another's burdens." Are there instances in which this principle has been co-opted? Are there those who have turned this into a "work of the flesh" and have made it into a sign of righteousness (like circumcision)?

Bibliography

Philippians

Bakirtzis, Charalambos, and Helmut Koester, eds. *Philippi at the Time of Paul and after His Death*. Harrisburg, Pennsylvania: Trinity Press International, 1998.

Bauckham, Richard J. "The Worship of Jesus in Philippians 2:9–11," in Ralph P. Martin and Brian J. Dodd, eds. *Where Christology Began: Essays on Philippians 2*. Louisville, Ky: Westminster John Knox Press, 1998, pp. 128–139.

Bockmuehl, Markus. *The Epistle to the Philippians*. Black's New Testament Commentaries. Peabody, Mass.: Hendrickson Publishers, 1998.

Craddock, Fred. *Philippians*. Interpretation: A Bible Commentary for Teaching and Preaching. Atlanta: John Knox Press, 1985.

Georgi, Dieter. *Theocracy in Paul's Practice and Theology* (translated by David Green). Minneapolis: Fortress Press, 1991.

Hawthorne, Gerald F. *Philippians*. The Word Biblical Commentary 43. Waco, Tex.: Word Books, 1983.

Horsley, Richard A., ed. *Paul and Empire. Religion and Power in Roman Imperial Society*. Harrisburg, Pennsylvania: Trinity Press International, 1997.

MacMullen, Ramsey. *Roman Social Relations*. New Haven, Conn.: Yale University Press, 1974.

Malina, Bruce. *The New Testament World: Insights from Cultural Anthropology*. Louisville, Ky.: Westminster John Knox Press, third edition, 2001.

Malina, Bruce. "Patron and Client. The Analogy Behind Synoptic Theology," *Forum* 4:1 (1988), republished in *The Social World of Jesus and the Gospels*. London and New York: Routledge, 1996, pp. 143–75.

Meeks, Wayne A. "The Man from Heaven in Paul's Letter to the Philippians," in Birger Pearson, ed., *The Future of Early Christianity: Essays in Honor of Helmut Koester*. Minneapolis: Fortress Press, 1991, pp. 329–36.

Meyer, Paul W., "The Worm at the Core of the Apple: Exegetical Reflections on Romans 7," in Robert T. Fortna and Beverly R. Gaventa, eds., *The Conversation Continues: Studies in Paul and John in Honor of J. Louis Martyn*. Nashville: Abingdon Press, 1990, pp. 62–84.

Murphy-O'Connor, Jerome. *Paul the Letter-Writer. His World, His Options, His Skills*. Collegeville, Minn.: Michael Glazier/The Liturgical Press, 1995.

Osiek, Carolyn. *Philippians, Philemon*. Abingdon New Testament Commentaries. Nashville: Abingdon Press, 2000.

Perkins, Pheme. "Philippians: Theology for the Heavenly Politeuma," in Jouette M. Bassler, ed. *Pauline Theology, Vol.1: Thessalonians, Philippians, Galatians, Philemon*. Minneapolis: Fortress Press, 1991.

Stowers, Stanley K. "Friends and Enemies in the Politics of Heaven. Reading Theology in Philippians," in Jouette M. Bassler, ed., *Pauline Theology: Vol 1: Thessalonians, Philippians, Galatians, Philemon*. Minneapolis: Fortress Press, 1991, pp. 105–21.

Wengst, Klaus. *Humility: Solidarity with the Humiliated*. (Translated by John Bowden from the German *Demut-Solidarität der Gedemütigten*. Munich: Christian Kaiser Verlag, 1987.) Philadelphia: Fortress Press, 1988.

Wengst, Klaus. *Pax Romana and the Peace of Jesus Christ*. (Translated by John Bowden.) Philadelphia: Fortress Press, 1987.

Witherington, Ben. *Friendship and Finances in Philippi. The Letter of Paul to the Philippians*. Valley Forge: Trinity Press International, 1994.

Galatians

Bassler, Jouette M. *Divine Impartiality: Paul and a Theological Axiom*. SBL Dissertation Series 59. Chico, Calif.: Scholars Press, 1982.

Betz, Hans Dieter. *Galatians*. Hermeneia. Philadelphia: Fortress Press, 1979.

Cousar, Charles B. *Galatians*. Interpretation: A Bible Commentary for Teaching and Preaching. Atlanta: John Knox Press, 1982.

Esler, Philip F. *Galatians* (New Testament Readings). London and New York: Routledge, 1998.

Lampe, Peter. "The Eucharist: Identifying with Christ on the Cross." *Interpretation* 48 (January 1994): 36–49.

Georgi, Dieter. *Remembering the Poor: The History of Paul's Collection for Jerusalem*. Nashville: Abingdon Press, 1992.

Longenecker, Bruce W. *The Triumph of Abraham's God: the Transformation of Identity in Galatians*. Nashville: Abingdon Press, 1998.

Malina, Bruce. *The New Testament World: Insights from Cultural Anthropology*. Louisville, Ky.: Westminster John Knox Press, third ed., 2001.

Martyn, J. Louis. *Galatians*. The Anchor Bible Commentary 33A. New York: Doubleday, 1997.

Murphy-O'Connor, Jerome. *Paul the Letter-Writer. His World, His Options, His Skills*. Collegeville, Minn.: Michael Glazier/The Liturgical Press, 1995.

Osiek, Carolyn, and Balch, David L. *Families in the New Testament World: Households and House Churches*. Louisville, Ky.: Westminster John Knox Press, 1997.

Stark, Rodney. *The Rise of Christianity*. San Francisco: HarperCollins, 1997.

Veyne, Paul. "The Roman Empire." *A History of Private Life: I. From Pagan Rome to Byzantium*. Arthur Goldhammer, translator. Cambridge, Mass.: The Belknap Press of Harvard University Press, 1987, pp. 5–234.

Wink, Walter. *Engaging the Powers: Discernment and Resistance in a World of Domination*. Minneapolis: Fortress Press, 1992.

Interpretation Bible Studies Leader's Guide

Interpretation Bible Studies (IBS), for adults and older youth, are flexible, attractive, easy-to-use, and filled with solid information about the Bible. IBS helps Christians discover the guidance and power of the scriptures for living today. Perhaps you are leading a church school class, a midweek Bible study group, or a youth group meeting, or simply using this in your own personal study. Whatever the setting may be, we hope you find this *Leader's Guide* helpful. Since every context and group is different, this *Leader's Guide* does not presume to tell you how to structure Bible study for your situation. Instead, the *Leader's Guide* seeks to offer choices—a number of helpful suggestions for leading a successful Bible study using IBS.

> "The church that no longer hears the essential message of the Scriptures soon ceases to understand what it is for and is open to be captured by the dominant religious philosophy of the moment."—James D. Smart, *The Strange Silence of the Bible in the Church: A Study in Hermeneutics* (Philadelphia: Westminster Press, 1970), 10.

How Should I Teach IBS?

1. Explore the Format

There is a wealth of information in IBS, perhaps more than you can use in one session. In this case, more is better. IBS has been designed to give you a well-stocked buffet of content and teachable insights. Pick and choose what suits your group's needs. Perhaps you will want to split units into two or more sessions, or combine units into a single session. Perhaps you will decide to use only a portion of a unit and then move on to the next unit. *There is not a structured theme or teaching focus to each unit that must be followed for IBS to be used.* Rather, IBS offers the flexibility to adjust to whatever suits your context.

A recent survey of both professional and volunteer church educators revealed that their number one concern was that Bible study materials be teacher-friendly. IBS is, indeed teacher-friendly in two important ways. First, since IBS provides abundant content and a flexible design, teachers can shape the lessons creatively, responding to the needs of the group and employing a wide variety of teaching methods. Second, those who wish more specific suggestions for planning the sessions can find them at the Geneva Press web site on the Internet (**www.ppcpub.org**). Click the "IBS Teacher Helps" button to access teaching suggestions for each IBS unit as well as helpful quotations, selections from Bible dictionaries and encyclopedias, and other teaching helps.

> "The more we bring to the Bible, the more we get from the Bible." —William Barclay, *A Beginner's Guide to the New Testament* (Louisville, Ky.: Westminster John Knox Press, 1995), vii.

IBS is not only teacher-friendly, it is also discussion-friendly. Given the opportunity, most adults and young people relish the chance to talk about the kind of issues raised in IBS. The secret, then, is to determine what works with your group, what will get them to talk. Several good methods for stimulating discussion are presented in this *Leader's Guide,* and once you learn your group, you can apply one of these methods and get the group discussing the Bible and its relevance in their lives.

The format of every IBS unit consists of several features:

a. Body of the Unit. This is the main content, consisting of interesting and informative commentary on the passage and scholarly insight into the biblical text and its significance for Christians today.

b. Sidebars. These are boxes that appear scattered throughout the body of the unit, with maps, photos, quotations, and intriguing ideas. Some sidebars can be identified quickly by a symbol, or icon, that helps the reader know what type of information can be found in that sidebar. There are icons for illustrations, key terms, pertinent quotes, and more.

c. Want to Know More? Each unit includes a "Want to Know More?" section that guides learners who wish to dig deeper and consult other resources. If your church library does not have the resources mentioned, you can look up the information in other standard Bible dictionaries, encyclopedias, and handbooks, or you can find much of this information at the Geneva Press Web site (see last page of this Guide).

d. Questions for Reflection. The unit ends with questions to help the learners think more deeply about the biblical passage and its pertinence for today. These questions are provided as examples only, and teachers are encouraged both to develop their own list of questions and to gather questions from the group. These discussion questions do not usually have specific "correct" answers. Again, the flexibility of IBS allows you to use these questions at the end of the group time, at the beginning, interspersed throughout, or not at all.

> "The trick is to make the Bible our book."—Duncan S. Ferguson, *Bible Basics: Mastering the Content of the Bible* (Louisville, Ky.: Westminster John Knox Press, 1995), 3.

2. Select a Teaching Method

Here are ten suggestions. The format of IBS allows you to choose what direction you will take as you plan to teach. Only you will know how your lesson should best be designed for your group. Some adult groups prefer the lecture method, while others prefer a high level of free-ranging discussion. Many youth groups like interaction, activity, the use of music, and the chance to talk about their own experiences and feelings. Here is a list of a few possible approaches. Let your own creativity add to the list!

a. Let's Talk about What We've Learned. In this approach, all group members are requested to read the scripture passage and the IBS unit before the group meets. Ask the group members to make notes about the main issues, concerns, and questions they see in the passage. When the group meets, these notes are collected, shared, and discussed. This method depends, of course, on the group's willingness to do some "homework."

b. What Do We Want and Need to Know? This approach begins by having the whole group read the scripture passage together. Then, drawing from your study of the IBS, you, as the teacher, write on a board or flip chart two lists:

(1) Things we should know to better understand this passage (content information related to the passage, for example, historical insights about political contexts, geographical landmarks, economic nuances, etc.), and

(2) Four or five "important issues we should talk about regarding this passage" (with implications for today— how the issues in the biblical context continue into today, for example, issues of idolatry or fear).

> "Although small groups can meet for many purposes and draw upon many different resources, the one resource which has shaped the life of the Church more than any other throughout its long history has been the Bible." —Roberta Hestenes, *Using the Bible in Groups* (Philadelphia: Westminster Press, 1983), 14.

Allow the group to add to either list, if they wish, and use the lists to lead into a time of learning, reflection, and discussion. This approach is suitable for those settings where there is little or no advanced preparation by the students.

c. Hunting and Gathering. Start the unit by having the group read the scripture passage together. Then divide the group into smaller clusters (perhaps having as few as one person), each with a different assignment. Some clusters can discuss one or more of the "Questions for Reflection." Others can look up key terms or people in a Bible dictionary or track down other biblical references found in the body of the unit. After the small clusters have had time to complete their tasks, gather the entire group again and lead them through the study material, allowing each cluster to contribute what it learned.

d. From Question Mark to Exclamation Point. This approach begins with contemporary questions and then moves to the biblical content as a response to those questions. One way to do this is for you to ask the group, at the beginning of the class, a rephrased version of one or more of the "Questions for Reflection" at the end of the study unit. For example, one of the questions at the end of the unit on Exodus 3:1–4:17 in the IBS *Exodus* volume reads,

> Moses raised four protests, or objections, to God's call. Contemporary people also raise objections to God's call. In what ways are these similar to Moses' protests? In what ways are they different?

This question assumes familiarity with the biblical passage about Moses, so the question would not work well before the group has explored the passage. However, try rephrasing this question as an opening exercise; for example:

Here is a thought experiment: Let's assume that God, who called people in the Bible to do daring and risky things, still calls people today to tasks of faith and courage. In the Bible, God called Moses from a burning bush and called Isaiah in a moment of ecstatic worship in the Temple. How do you think God's call is experienced by people today? Where do you see evidence of people saying "yes" to God's call? When people say "no" or raise an objection to God's call, what reasons do they give (to themselves, to God)?

Posing this or a similar question at the beginning will generate discussion and raise important issues, and then it can lead the group into an exploration of the biblical passage as a resource for thinking even more deeply about these questions.

e. Let's Go to the Library. From your church library, your pastor's library, or other sources, gather several good commentaries on the book of the Bible you are studying. Among the trustworthy commentaries are those in the Interpretation series (John Knox Press) and the Westminster Bible Companion series (Westminster John Knox Press). Divide your group into smaller clusters and give one commentary to each cluster (one or more of the clusters can be given the IBS volume instead of a full-length commentary). Ask each cluster to read the biblical passage you are studying and then to read the section of the commentary that covers that passage (if your group is large, you may want to make photocopies of the commentary material with proper permission, of course). The task of each cluster is to name the two or three most important insights they discover about the biblical passage by reading and talking together about the commentary material. When you reassemble the larger group to share these insights, your group will gain not only a variety of insights about the passage but also a sense that differing views of the same text are par for the course in biblical interpretation.

f. Working Creatively Together. Begin with a creative group task, tied to the main thrust of the study. For example, if the study is on the Ten Commandments, a parable, or a psalm, have the group rewrite the Ten Commandments, the parable, or the psalm in contemporary language. If the passage is an epistle, have the group write a letter to their own congregation. Or if the study is a narrative, have the group role-play the characters in the story or write a page describing the story from the point of view of one of the characters. After completion of the task, read and discuss the biblical passage, asking for interpretations and applications from the group and tying in IBS material as it fits the flow of the discussion.

g. Singing Our Faith. Begin the session by singing (or reading) together a hymn that alludes to the biblical passage being studied (or to the theological themes in the passage). Most hymnals have an index of scriptural allusions. For example, if you are studying the unit from the IBS volume on Psalm 121, you can sing "I to the Hills Will Lift My Eyes," "Sing Praise to God, Who Reigns Above," or another hymn based on Psalm 121. Let the group reflect on the thoughts and feelings evoked by the hymn, then move to the biblical passage, allowing the biblical text and the IBS material to underscore, clarify, refine, and deepen the discussion stimulated by the hymn. If you are ambitious, you may ask the group to write a new hymn at the end of the study! (Many hymnals have indexes in the back or companion volumes that help the user match hymns to scripture passages or topics.)

h. Fill in the Blanks. In order to help the learners focus on the content of the biblical passage, at the beginning of the session ask each member of the group to read the biblical passage and fill out a brief questionnaire about the details of the passage (provide a copy for each learner or write the questions on the board). For example, if you are studying the unit in the IBS *Matthew* volume on Matthew 22:1–14, the questionnaire could include questions such as the following:

—In this story, Jesus compares the kingdom of heaven to what?
—List the various responses of those who were invited to the king's banquet but who did not come.
—When his invitation was rejected, how did the king feel? What did the king do?
—In the second part of the story, when the king saw a man at the banquet without a wedding garment, what did the king say? What did the man say? What did the king do?
—What is the saying found at the end of this story?

Gather the group's responses to the questions and perhaps encourage discussion. Then lead the group through the IBS material helping the learners to understand the meanings of these details and the significance of the passage for today. Feeling creative? Instead of a fill-in-the blanks questionnaire, create a crossword puzzle from names and words in the biblical passage.

i. Get the Picture. In this approach, stimulate group discussion by incorporating a painting, photograph, or other visual object into the lesson. You can begin by having the group examine and comment on this visual or you can introduce the visual later in the lesson—it depends on the object used. If, for example, you are studying the unit Exodus 3:1–4:17 in the IBS *Exodus* volume, you may want to view Paul Koli's very colorful painting *The Burning Bush.* Two sources for this painting are *The Bible Through Asian Eyes,* edited by Masao Takenaka and Ron O'Grady (National City, Calif.: Pace Publishing Co., 1991), and *Imaging the Word: An Arts and Lectionary Resource,* vol. 3, edited by Susan A. Blain (Cleveland: United Church Press, 1996).

j. Now Hear This. Especially if your class is large, you may want to use the lecture method. As the teacher, you prepare a presentation on the biblical passage, using as many resources as you have available plus your own experience, but following the content of the IBS unit as a guide. You can make the lecture even more lively by asking the learners at various points along the way to refer to the visuals and quotes found in the "sidebars." A place can be made for questions (like the ones at the end of the unit)—either at the close of the lecture or at strategic points along the way.

> "It is . . . important to call a Bible study group back to what the text being discussed actually says, especially when an individual has gotten off on some tangent." —Richard Robert Osmer, *Teaching for Faith: A Guide for Teachers of Adult Classes* (Louisville, Ky.: Westminster John Knox Press, 1992), 71.

3. Keep These Teaching Tips in Mind

There are no surefire guarantees for a teaching success. However, the following suggestions can increase the chances for a successful study:

a. Always Know Where the Group Is Headed. Take ample time beforehand to prepare the material. Know the main points of the study, and know the destination. Be flexible, and encourage discussion, but don't lose sight of where you are headed.

b. Ask Good Questions; Don't Be Afraid of Silence. Ideally, a discussion blossoms spontaneously from the reading of the scripture. But more often than not, a discussion must be drawn from the group members by a series of well-chosen questions. After asking each question, give the group members time to answer. Let them think, and don't be threatened by a season of silence. Don't feel that every question must have an answer, and that as leader, you must supply every answer. Facilitate discussion by getting the group members to cooperate with each other. Sometimes, the original question can be restated. Sometimes it is helpful to ask a follow-up question like "What makes this a hard question to answer?"

Ask questions that encourage explanatory answers. Try to avoid questions that can be answered simply "Yes" or "No." Rather than asking, "Do you think Moses was frightened by the burning bush?" ask, "What do you think Moses was feeling and experiencing as he stood before the burning bush?" If group members answer with just one word, ask a follow-up question like "Why do you think this is so?" Ask questions about their feelings and opinions, mixed within questions about facts or details. Repeat their responses or restate their response to reinforce their contributions to the group.

> "Studies of learning reveal that while people remember approximately 10% of what they hear, they remember up to 90% of what they say. Therefore, to increase the amount of learning that occurs, increase the amount of talking about the Bible which each member does."—Roberta Hestenes, *Using the Bible in Groups* (Philadelphia: Westminster Press, 1983), 17.

Most studies can generate discussion by asking open-ended questions. Depending on the group, several types of questions can work. Some groups will respond well to content questions that can be answered from reading the IBS comments or the biblical passage. Others will respond well to questions about feelings or thoughts. Still others will respond to questions that challenge them to new thoughts or that may not have exact answers. Be sensitive to the group's dynamic in choosing questions.

Some suggested questions are: What is the point of the passage? Who are the main characters? Where is the tension in the story? Why does it say (this)_____, and not (that) _____? What raises questions for you? What terms need defining? What are the new ideas? What doesn't make sense? What bothers or troubles you about this passage? What keeps you from living the truth of this passage?

c. Don't Settle for the Ordinary. There is nothing like a surprise. Think of special or unique ways to present the ideas of the study. Upset the applecart of the ordinary. Even though the passage may be familiar, look for ways to introduce suspense. Remember that a little mystery can capture the imagination. Change your routine.

Along with the element of surprise, humor can open up a discussion. Don't be afraid to laugh. A well-chosen joke or cartoon may present the central theme in a way that a lecture would have stymied.

Sometimes a passage is too familiar. No one speaks up because everyone feels that all that could be said has been said. Choose an unfamiliar translation from which to read, or if the passage is from a Gospel, compare the story across two or more Gospels and note differences. It is amazing what insights can be drawn from seeing something strange in what was thought to be familiar.

d. Feel Free to Supplement the IBS Resources with Other Material. Consult other commentaries or resources. Tie in current events with the lesson. Scour newspapers or magazines for stories that touch on the issues of the study. Sometimes the lyrics of a song, or a section of prose from a well-written novel will be just the right seasoning for the study.

e. And Don't Forget to Check the Web. Check out our site on the World Wide Web (www.ppcpub.org). Click the "IBS Teacher Helps" button to access teaching suggestions. Several possibilities for applying the teaching methods suggested above for individual IBS units will be available. Feel free to download this material.

> "The Bible is literature, but it is much more than literature. It is the holy book of Jews and Christians, who find there a manifestation of God's presence." —Kathleen Norris, *The Psalms* (New York: Riverhead Books, 1997), xxii.

f. Stay Close to the Biblical Text. Don't forget that the goal is to learn the Bible. Return to the text again and again. Avoid making the mistake of reading the passage only at the beginning of the study, and then wandering away to comments on top of comments from that point on. Trust in the power and presence of the Holy Spirit to use the truths of the passage to work within the lives of the study participants.

What If I Am Using IBS in Personal Bible Study?

If you are using IBS in your personal Bible study, you can experiment and explore a variety of ways. You may choose to read straight through the study without giving any attention to the sidebars or other features. Or you may find yourself interested in a question or unfamiliar with a key term, and you can allow the sidebars "Want to Know More?" and "Questions for Reflection" to lead you into deeper learning on these issues. Perhaps you will want to have a few commentaries or a Bible dictionary available to pursue what interests you. As was suggested in one of the teaching methods above, you may want to begin with the questions at the end, and then read the Bible passage followed by the IBS material. Trust the IBS resources to provide good and helpful information, and then follow your interests!

Want to Know More?

About leading Bible study groups? See Roberta Hestenes, *Using the Bible in Groups* (Philadelphia: Westminster Press, 1983); Christine Blair, *The Art of Teaching the Bible* (Louisville, Ky.: Geneva Press, 2001).

About basic Bible content? See Duncan S. Ferguson, *Bible Basics: Mastering the Content of the Bible* (Louisville, Ky.: Westminster John Knox Press, 1995); William M. Ramsay, *The Westminster Guide to the Books of the Bible* (Louisville, Ky.: Westminster John Knox Press, 1994).

About the development of the Bible? See John Barton, *How the Bible Came to Be* (Louisville, Ky.: Westminster John Knox Press, 1997).

About the meaning of difficult terms? See Donald K. McKim, *Westminster Dictionary of Theological Terms* (Louisville, Ky.: Westminster John Knox Press, 1996); Paul J. Achtemeier, *Harper's Bible Dictionary* (San Francisco: Harper & Row, 1985).

For more information about IBS,
click the "IBS Teacher Helps" button at
www.ppcpub.org